HANDSOME RANSOM JACKSON

HANDSOME RANSOM JACKSON

Accidental Big Leaguer

Ransom Jackson

with Gaylon H. White

ROWMAN & LITTLEFIELD
Lanham • Boulder • New York • London

Published by Rowman & Littlefield
A wholly owned subsidary of The Rowman & Littlefield Publishing Group,
Inc.
4501 Forbes Boulevard, Suite 200, Lanham, Maryland 20706
www.rowman.com

Unit A, Whitacre Mews, 26-34 Stannary Street, London SE11 4AB

British Library Cataloguing in Publication Information Available

Names: Jackson, Ransom, 1926– | White, Gaylon H., 1946–
Title: Handsome Ransom Jackson : accidental Big Leaguer / Ransom Jackson Jr. with Gaylon H.
     White.
Description: Lanham : ROWMAN & LITTLEFIELD, [2016] | Includes bibliographical refer-
     ences and index.
Identifiers: LCCN 2015035524| ISBN 9781442261549 (hardcover : alk. paper) | ISBN
     9781442261556 (ebook)
Subjects: LCSH: Jackson, Ransom, 1926– | Baseball players—United States—Biography.
Classification: LCC GV865.J3 A3 2016 | DDC 796.357092--dc23 LC record available at http://
     lccn.loc.gov/2015035524

∞ ™ The paper used in this publication meets the minimum requirements of
American National Standard for Information Sciences Permanence of Paper
for Printed Library Materials, ANSI/NISO Z39.48-1992.

Printed in the United States of America

This book is a labor of love for my wife, Terry, and our family, as they were either too young or not yet born to have experienced some of this adventure with me. I have put these stories on paper so they can be enjoyed and remembered by our six children and their spouses: Randy and wife, Laurie; Chuck and wife, Anna; Ann and husband, Clay; Ginny and husband, Bill; Meredith and husband, Kenny; Ransom and wife, Lara; twelve grandchildren and their spouses: Courtney and husband, Bill; Rachel; Leeanne and husband, Dustin; Trey and wife, Ashley; Emily; Alison; Paige; Fowler; Luke; Wells; Elizabeth, and Levi; and so far six great grandchildren: Madison, Harrison, Savannah, Marshall, Kristopher, and Jackson. You're all stars in my book.
—Ransom Jackson Jr.

A tip of my Cubs baseball hat to my mother, Mildred Joyce White, who didn't throw away my collection of ten thousand baseball cards when I left home for college. She preserved all of them, including my "Handsome Ransom" Jackson cards, as if they were diamonds. That's a loving mother, deserving of a baseball card of her own.
—Gaylon H. White

CONTENTS

viii

CONTENTS

FOREWORD

Roger Craig

The first time I walked in the Brooklyn Dodgers clubhouse in 1955 and saw all of the team's great players, I thought to myself, "I don't belong."

Wherever I looked there was a future Hall of Famer: Jackie Robinson, Roy Campanella, Pee Wee Reese, and Duke Snider. There also was Gil Hodges, Carl Furillo, Jim Gilliam, Don Newcombe, and Carl Erskine—superstars on any other team.

Randy Jackson was a two-time All-Star when he joined the Dodgers in 1956 so he didn't have the same doubts I did. He played against these guys with the Chicago Cubs. Now they were his teammates and the Dodgers tabbed him to replace one of them—Jackie Robinson.

Jackie wasn't the legend he is today. The number, forty-two, was still on his back, not yet retired and displayed prominently in every big-league ballpark in America. There were questions about Jackie's future but not the greatness of his accomplishments since breaking Major League Baseball's color barrier in 1947.

It's hard to imagine now the pressure of replacing Jackie at third base. He was thirty-seven and trying to rebound from a career-worst year but he was Jackie, the greatest player and most tenacious competitor that ever lived.

All eyes were on Jackie and Randy at spring training. I had a front row seat, so to speak, because I was Randy's roommate. If he was bothered by the pressure, it never showed.

As a hitter, Randy was a tough out. He made all of the plays on defense. He worked hard.

Randy sat on the bench for nearly two months. He never complained. When Jackie went into a batting slump, Randy moved into the starting lineup, batting cleanup behind Snider. He was one of the hottest hitters in the National League until he was injured in a freak household accident.

Randy was the same through these ups and downs. In fact, he had a calming effect on me.

I had a 12–11 won-loss record in 1956, winning eight of my first ten decisions. I lost my next two games, the second a 2–0 loss. "Hey, you pitched your heart out," Randy said. "We didn't score any runs."

Randy kept me positive, never letting me get negative. That carried me the rest of my career, especially the next two years.

I hurt my right arm pitching the last game in Brooklyn Dodger history—September 29, 1957. In the seventh inning I threw a curveball and felt something snap in my shoulder. I was taken out for a pinch hitter the following inning and didn't tell anybody about my arm except for my wife, Carolyn. "This was the last game of the season," I said. "It will be okay next spring."

It never was. I found out later it was a torn rotator cuff. Today, there's Tommy John surgery to make a pitcher's bad arm feel good again. At the time the surgical procedure was as unknown as Tommy John, the Dodger pitcher who made it famous.

I had to learn how to pitch again. My good fastball was gone but I ended up mastering two other pitches, a sinker and a slider. Staying positive was the key to making the transition and staying in the majors another nine seasons.

The first game I pitched for the Dodgers in 1955 is also noteworthy because it provides insight into Jackie and his replacement, Randy.

I was in the Ebbets Field locker room after pitching a three-hitter to beat the Cincinnati Redlegs, 6–2. Dodger manager Walter Alston came up to me and said, "Kid, you have a wife and baby in Montreal. Why don't you go back and pick them up?"

I was with the Montreal Royals in the International League prior to joining the Dodgers. I grew up in North Carolina. This was my first time in New York City and I didn't have a clue about how to get to Idlewild Airport (now John F. Kennedy).

"Go to the underground and catch the train," somebody said.

"What do you mean go underground? What am I going to do there?"

"That's where you catch the train."

"They don't have trains underground."

On hearing this, Jackie came to my rescue.

"Come on, kid, I'll give you a ride to the airport."

I was nervous and scared when I got in the car. Jackie immediately put me at ease.

"You've got a chance to be a good major-league pitcher," he said, "and here are some things you need to learn."

I found out later that Jackie didn't live near the airport. He went out of his way to take me there.

That brings me back to Randy.

He was the perfect roommate, a fun guy to be around. Like Jackie, he was a class act, a role model for younger players like me. The tips they gave stuck with me my entire career. Randy was the right guy to replace Jackie because their character and lifestyle was Hall of Fame.

Roger Craig is a former major-league pitcher, coach, and manager. In twelve seasons, he won seventy-four games for the Dodgers, New York Mets, St. Louis Cardinals, and Philadelphia Phillies. As a coach, his specialty was teaching the split-finger fastball to pitchers for the San Diego Padres, Houston Astros, and Detroit Tigers. He managed the San Diego Padres in 1978–1979 and the San Francisco Giants from 1985 to 1992, leading them to the National League pennant in 1989.

PREFACE

The working title for the first draft of this book was *A Mighty Lucky Guy*.

Even though the title wasn't used, it still describes my life in sports, a series of lucky events far beyond my wildest dreams. I feel even luckier as the years pass and many of the guys I played with and against pass away.

Within the span of one month in 2015, two Chicago icons died. First it was Ernie "Mr. Cub" Banks, and then Orestes "Minnie" Minoso, also known as "The Cuban Comet" and "Mr. White Sox." I played alongside Ernie three full seasons and part of a fourth with the Cubs. Minnie was a teammate with the Cleveland Indians in 1958–59.

A month later we said goodbye to Al Rosen, a star third baseman for the Indians in the early 1950s. We played against each other in the 1954 and 1955 Major League Baseball All-Star Games.

On September 22, 2015, Yogi Berra died. Not only was he one of the greatest catchers to play the game, he was a cultural icon with his Yogisms that cut across generations because they bring common sense to daily life.

"You can observe a lot by just watching," Yogi said. "It ain't over till it's over."

The deaths of these great ballplayers reminded me of how lucky I was to be on the same field with them and still be around to write about it.

I didn't play high school baseball or football, and yet I played big-league baseball for ten years and three seasons of college football, including back-to-back Cotton Bowl games for different schools—Texas Christian University (TCU) and the University of Texas. This was the first and only time that will happen as athletes who transfer colleges now are required to sit out a year.

I was the last Brooklyn Dodger to hit a home run, although I didn't know this until it was a trivia question many years later on the television show *Good Morning America*.

When Major League Baseball started recording intentional walks in 1955, I was the first to receive one in the National League and perhaps all of baseball. Again, I didn't have a clue until long after I retired.

In football, I played for two Hall of Fame coaches—Leo Robert "Dutch" Meyer at TCU and Dana X. Bible at Texas. Meyer was my baseball coach at TCU, and Bibb Falk was my coach at Texas. Bibb replaced Shoeless Joe Jackson after the legendary outfielder was banned from baseball for his involvement in the Chicago Black Sox gambling scandal in the 1919 World Series.

A teammate at Texas in both football and baseball was Bobby Layne, a National Football League Hall of Fame quarterback who was hailed by *Sports Illustrated* in 1995 as the toughest to ever play that position.

I played baseball for two storied teams, the Chicago Cubs and the Dodgers, both in Brooklyn and Los Angeles. In Chicago, my primary workplace was Wrigley Field, a shrine as much as a ballpark. In Brooklyn, it was Ebbets Field, a cozy little stadium where fans in the stands were as entertaining as the players on the field.

In addition to Mr. Cub, I had the privilege of sharing the same locker room with Jackie Robinson, Duke Snider, Pee Wee Reese, Roy Campanella, Don Drysdale, Sandy Koufax, Ralph Kiner, Hoyt Wilhelm, Dick Williams, and Billy Williams, all members of the National Baseball Hall of Fame in Cooperstown, New York. Dodger manager Walter Alston is in the Hall of Fame as well as two other managers I played for, Frank Frisch in Chicago and Joe Gordon in Cleveland. Incidentally, Frisch didn't get there for his 141–196 record managing the Cubs.

Call it luck, serendipity, or a godsend, but one of them was responsible for my meeting Gaylon White, the writer who assisted me on this book. One of my wife's high school classmates hooked us up without knowing I was looking for help.

White was a perfect fit because he was born and raised in Los Angeles and a diehard baseball and Cub fan. He took a raw, sixty-page manuscript (typed single space), chock full of stories the way I tell them sitting in my easy chair at home, checked the facts for accuracy, and then polished and arranged them so they read exactly the way I lived them.

Near the end of the project, White shared a typed note sent to him in the early 1970s by a friend, Ed Cunningham. The note was inspired by a long conversation about baseball cards.

"I am bursting with nostalgia," Cunningham wrote. "It occurs to me that if one were to recite this litany of greats, near greats, and never greats each morning before breakfast, he would feel twenty years younger in two weeks. We ought to develop our own baseball chant. It might replace transcendental meditation!

"Do you remember the year Don Larsen won three and lost twenty-one?

"Do you remember Ewell "The Whip" Blackwell?

"Do you remember Dom DiMaggio? (I had a bat with his name on it.)

"Do you remember Skeeter Kell? Wilmer Shantz? Frank Baumholtz? (An ex-Chicagoite once told me that the very mention of that last name brought back his entire childhood. Why didn't Marcel Proust ever write a baseball book?)"

The note ended with this poem written by Cunningham after he read the lineups for the 1970 All-Star Game:

> Why is Hodges sidelined
> With a clipboard in his hands?
> What is Bobby Feller doing
> Sitting in the stands?
> Where have all my heroes gone?
> Where's Big Johnny Mize?
> Where's The Splinter?
> Where's The Man?
> Who are all these guys?

All of the guys mentioned in the poem are gone. Fortunately, we have the wonderful memories they left behind.

That's what this book is all about—one man's memories of a bygone era when baseball was really the national pastime and the nicknames of its stars could stand on their own: Stan the Man, the Splendid Splinter, the Cuban Comet, and Mr. Cub, to list a few.

I'm grateful my family urged me to write down all of the stories that would've been buried along with me.

They are fun stories like spring training with the Cubs on Catalina Island; befriending a Mafia boss in Springfield, Massachusetts; and batting behind Hank Sauer, the so-called Mayor of Wrigley Field, and getting knocked down by pitchers retaliating for home runs Sauer hit.

In 1956, I joined the Brooklyn Dodgers to take over at third base for the aging Jackie Robinson. As I soon discovered, nobody replaces a legend like Jackie, even if he was in a rocking chair.

My first roommate with the Dodgers was Roger Craig, a rangy right-handed pitcher from North Carolina who won twelve games in 1956 and went on to become a highly successful manager for the San Diego Padres and San Francisco Giants.

One of my other teammates in Brooklyn was a tall, talented pitcher with movie-star looks—Don Drysdale. We roomed together on a historic baseball tour of Japan in late 1956 and later sat in the dugout in L.A. looking for Hollywood celebrities in the stands.

I was lucky that some sportswriter tagged me Handsome Ransom, a nickname that rhymes and is easy to remember. Two of my three boys and one grandson are named Ransom. I know of three fans who named their sons after me. Two of them go by Ransom and the other Randy. His last name is Gandy so he's Randy Gandy.

One evening during spring training at Mesa, Arizona, in the early 1950s I went to the greyhound dog track. I was checking out the handicap form when I noticed a dog named Randy Jackson was running in the fourth race. The odds were fifty-to-one. I put down five dollars for Randy to win. There were eight dogs in the race and he finished last.

That wasn't a lucky night, but when I think about Randy Gandy and all the amazing things I've experienced, I realize what a lucky guy I am—lucky to be the right guy in the right place at the right time and, finally, lucky to still be alive to tell about it.

ACKNOWLEDGMENTS

I want to thank my family for encouraging me to put the story of my life on paper. I started two years ago with pen and legal pads and wound up with 312 pages. My wife, Terry, keypunched the handwritten notes into her computer so they would be easier to read.

I was extremely lucky to find Gaylon White, the best in the business for presenting my stories in the way you are going to read them. Gaylon is a friend of Ellis Smith, a high school friend of Terry's. He has a wealth of talent, knowledge, and experience in writing and was gracious enough to share that with me. I am forever grateful for his help, his suggestions, and his belief that what I had to say was something all baseball fans would enjoy reading. A special thanks to his wife, Mary, for sharing him with us during this endeavor.

In the early 1900s, the defensive wizardry of Chicago Cubs shortstop Joe Tinker, second baseman Johnny Evers, and first baseman Frank Chance inspired the poem "Baseball's Sad Lexicon," and the famous line "Tinker to Evers to Chance."

In 1954, the trio of Ernie Banks at short, Gene Baker at second, and Steve Bilko at first lifted Cubs play-by-play announcer Bert Wilson to new alliterative heights with "Bingo to Bango to Bilko."

It had a nice ring to it, but unfortunately Bilko spent most of the season on the bench, rendering the rhyme a useless piece of trivia until Gaylon adopted it to describe the teamwork that went into this book.

Gaylon spent many hours in research and sent hundreds of e-mails that with Terry's help, I responded to electronically. He set me up with

a digital recorder that enabled me to capture memories by simply push-
ing a button. This was how the "Bingo to Bango to Bilko" combination
was supposed to work.

I want to thank Brent Shyer of O'Malley Seidler Partners for providing valuable information on the Brooklyn Dodgers' visit to Japan in
1956.

Mark Langill of the Los Angeles Dodgers tracked down the photo of
me with other ex-Dodger third basemen taken at Dodger Stadium in
2008 to mark the team's fiftieth anniversary in L.A. Mark also contributed tidbits on Gladys Goodding, the organist at Brooklyn's Ebbets
Field, who, as Mark s aptly puts it, gave the Dodgers "the musical boot
out of town" in 1957.

Michael Graham, the nephew of one of my cousins, contributed the
photo of me with Duke Snider, Gil Hodges, and Roy Campanella.

Rosemary Morrow of Redux Pictures led our successful search for
the *New York Times* photo of Chicago Cub manager Frank Frisch reading a book in the dugout during a game in 1951. Thank you, Rosemary.

John Horne, photo archivist for the National Baseball Hall of Fame
and Museum in Cooperstown, helped secure the picture of Dodger
manager Walter Alston.

Cassidy Lent, a reference librarian at the Hall of Fame, provided
information needed to verify that I was the first player in National
League history to receive a recorded intentional base on balls.

Most of the newspaper articles cited are preserved in scrapbooks my
late father, Ransom Joseph Sr., compiled over the years. He probably
knew I'd need them some day.

We were able to track down the dates and page numbers for most of
the stories because of helpful folks like Tim Spindle of the Oklahoma
City Metropolitan Library System, Diane Parks of the Boston Public
Library, Laura Steinbach of the Texas Christian University Library, and
Vince Lee of the University of Houston Library.

There are a lot of names in this book. Leann DeBord hit a grand-
slam with an index that makes finding them simple.

I want to thank all of the baseball fans who have written me over the
years, often asking for my autograph. It's nice to be remembered.

Christen Karniski is far too young to have known much about me
before my manuscript arrived at Rowman & Littlefield, where she is an
associate editor. Fortunately, Christen liked what she read and made it

possible for a lot more people to enjoy these stories. Thanks also to her colleague, Kellie Hagan, senior production editor, for bringing everything together so well.

Most of all I want to thank my wife, Terry. Without her encouragement and hard work, all these stories would still be on a yellow legal pad.

INTRODUCTION

One of baseball's most enduring images is New York Yankees pitcher Don Larsen cradling catcher Yogi Berra in his arms after the last out of his perfect game in the 1956 World Series, the only one in Series history.

I watched from the bench with my Brooklyn Dodger teammates. We were the victims of Larsen's perfection in the fifth game at Yankee Stadium. The famous photograph is a painful reminder of our futility that day, and eventual loss of the series in seven games.

The image is everlasting, just like its central figure, Yogi Berra. Yogi died in 2015 but his quotes and stories live on, generating more tales like the one from a Yankees–Chicago Cubs exhibition game in 1951 at Phoenix Municipal Stadium.

I was with the Cubs at the time, waiting in the on-deck circle as Frank Baumholtz batted. Yogi was catching. When Baumholtz hit a fly ball to right field, Yogi ran the other way down the third-base line. Yogi was giggling when I got up to the plate.

"What's so funny?" I asked.

Yogi said he was running after the ball only to discover that it was a butterfly.

The image of Yogi chasing an imaginary butterfly is as vivid in my mind as Larsen holding him in his arms. Both symbolize the simplicity and innocence of baseball in the 1950s.

There was no ESPN to analyze and dissect every game.

There were no tell-all books so players didn't have to worry about their dirty laundry leaving the locker room.

Nobody had to worry about being politically correct because the term didn't exist.

The Internet had yet to be invented so there was no risk of embarrassing photos showing up on Facebook or a blog post. What happened in Chicago stayed in Chicago or the other twelve cities that had major-league teams in 1956. There were only sixteen teams, and Chicago and New York City had five of them—the Cubs, White Sox, Yankees, Giants, and Dodgers.

There was no free agency or agents. Players belonged to the team that signed them until they were released or traded to another team. Many talented players languished in the minors or on the bench of big-league teams. I batted .471 my first spring training with the Cubs in 1948 and was assigned to a Class A team in the minors.

Baseball was a family business with none of the corporate trappings of today. The Cubs were owned by the Wrigley family; the Dodgers by the O'Malley family; the St. Louis Cardinals by the Busch family.

The manager and front-office people often were friends of the family. The Cubs manager in 1948 was Charlie "Jolly Cholly" Grimm, a banjo-playing buddy of owner Philip K. Wrigley.

Most players had off-season jobs. I worked in my family's laundry business and, then, sold life insurance.

Fans could easily relate to players because, off the field, we were regular guys. Our names were usually listed in the telephone book. Most of us didn't have expensive homes or drive fancy cars. When I played for the Brooklyn Dodgers, I lived in an apartment and took the subway to and from work at Ebbets Field.

More than a half century has passed since I played my last game and people still ask for my autograph.

At one baseball card show I sat next to Morganna Roberts, the amply endowed exotic dancer known as "The Kissing Bandit" because of all the times she ran onto the field to kiss baseball and football players. Instead of a kiss, she gave me a color photo signed "Breast wishes, Morganna."

I was treated like a star and, yet, I never felt like one until some people started confusing me with Randy Jackson, a judge on the television show *American Idol*.

I was one of the lucky few to get paid for playing a boy's game well past my boyhood.

Maybe that's why I find the image of Yogi and the butterfly so appealing and just as enduring as the iconic shot of Yogi and Larsen. As great a player as Yogi was, he could laugh at himself for mistaking a butterfly for a baseball.

The stories in this book are meant to preserve some of my own personal experiences as well as a sliver of history from college football in the mid-1940s and the heart of the golden era of baseball in the 1950s. I broke into the majors in 1950 and played my last game in 1959 so my career spanned the entire decade.

The fifties changed baseball forever and for the better.

Going into 1950, only four of the sixteen teams were integrated. By 1960, black players were on every club's roster.

The fifties introduced Hank Aaron, Ernie Banks, Orlando Cepeda, Roberto Clemente, Curt Flood, Elston Howard, Willie Mays, Willie McCovey, Frank Robinson, and Billy Williams—black and Latino stars who not only changed the way the game is played but how it operates as a business. Mays was a free spirit on the diamond with his basket catches in center field and running out from under his cap on the base paths. Flood, also a center fielder, challenged baseball's reserve clause, leading to its eventual demise and the free agency that gives today's players the flexibility to make the most of their ability.

The landscape for the big leagues also changed dramatically. The Braves moved from Boston to Milwaukee in 1953; the Browns from St. Louis to Baltimore in 1954 where they became the Orioles; the Athletics from Philadelphia to Kansas City, Missouri, in 1955; and the biggest move of all in 1958, the Dodgers from Brooklyn to Los Angeles and the Giants from New York City to San Francisco. This triggered the westward expansion in the 1960s when new franchises were added in Los Angeles (Angels), San Diego (Padres), and Seattle (Pilots) and the Athletics relocated to Oakland.

The only two ballparks remaining from the fifties are Chicago's Wrigley Field and Boston's Fenway Park. The rest exist only in movie footage and the minds of players and fans who set foot in them. "The ballparks that are gone have the charm of being gone," historian John Thorn said in the film *The Lost Ballparks of Major League Baseball*. "There's something wonderful about being lost."[1]

As I watched the movie *42* about Jackie Robinson breaking organized baseball's color barrier in 1947, my focus was on the fences and the backgrounds of the three ballparks featured—Brooklyn's Ebbets Field; St. Louis's Sportsman's Park, and Cincinnati's Crosley Field. I wanted to see how close they came to the real thing. Only Ebbets Field passed the test.

Lost in all of the nostalgia that shrouds the old ballparks is that the empty seats often outnumbered the fans.

There were so few people (3,392) in the stands at Boston's Braves Field for a game in 1950 that I could hear them talking from my position at third base.

The Dodgers' last game at Ebbets Field was witnessed by a mere 6,702 fans.

The average attendance for a game at Wrigley Field during my seven years with the Cubs was 11,418, about a third of what the Cubs currently average.

The crowds are bigger; the new ballparks are better; the players bigger, stronger, and better paid; and the game different. Things like the designated hitter, pitch counts, and relief pitchers for every type of situation have changed how the game is played.

There are still some amazing players in baseball, but I wonder if any of them will become as legendary as Henry Aaron, Willie Mays, Mickey Mantle, and other greats from the fifties.

I'm almost certain there will never be another Yogi Berra. Even if someone like Yogi did come along, it would be like Dale Berra once said about comparisons with his father, "Our similarities are different."

Part I

Early Years and the Minor Leagues

I

RANSOM AS IN HANDSOME

They called me Handsome Ransom. The nickname has less to do with looks and more to do with a sportswriter looking for something to rhyme with Ransom.

As baseball nicknames go, it's not bad. Old-timers who remember nothing else about my ten years with the Chicago Cubs, Brooklyn/Los Angeles Dodgers, and Cleveland Indians can probably recall Handsome Ransom because it rhymes and, well, it's different. At baseball card shows long after I retired, I was often asked to sign my name Handsome Ransom Jackson. But it can be embarrassing.

At six foot one and 170-something pounds, there wasn't much of a chance of being confused physically with Gorgeous George, the flamboyant pro wrestler who was famous in the 1950s. But I didn't want to get body slammed by someone thinking I was a cocky, boastful athlete. I was actually a quiet, shy guy, far more comfortable with a baseball bat doing my talking.

When you think about it, the baseball bat is a marvelous communications tool. The cracking sound of a bat making contact with a ball is a statement. A hard-hit ball sends a message of authority. The results are measured by statistics such as hits, runs batted in, and batting average. The numbers require no explanation. They speak for themselves.

My numbers were good enough to earn me two trips to the All-Star Game, the annual showcase of big-league baseball's best players. I had 835 hits, including 103 home runs; batted in 415 runs in 955 games; and posted a .261 average. Nothing spectacular. But not too shabby considering I played during the golden era of baseball when there were only sixteen teams and pitchers like Warren Spahn and Johnny Sain were so good that there was a saying, "Spahn and Sain, and pray for rain." I didn't hit a home run off either of them, but I belted four off of Don Newcombe and three against Carl Erskine when I was with the Cubs and they were the aces of the Brooklyn Dodgers pitching staff. I also batted .333—1-for-3—against the Dodgers' Sandy Koufax. He's enshrined at the National Baseball Hall of Fame in Cooperstown, New York; I'm not.

I didn't know anything about Cooperstown or baseball growing up in Little Rock, Arkansas.

I was born February 10, 1926, to Ransom Joseph and Ann Polk Coolidge Jackson. He was from Hamburg in the southern part of Arkansas near the Louisiana border. She was a society queen from Helena, a town about seventy miles down the Mississippi River from Memphis, Tennessee. They got married in Helena in 1923, the local newspaper devoting a full page to the wedding. The only mention of Dad was in the last sentence of the story: "The groom has travelled extensively."

Dad attended the University of Virginia for two years and then transferred to Princeton University in New Jersey where the next two years he combined his studies with playing varsity baseball. On graduating in 1922, he went into the cotton brokerage business with his brother, Bruin, and Harry Hill, a brother-in-law. They had offices in New York City, London, and Paris.

The business prospered, Dad drawing a salary of $250,000, which was a lot of money in those days. He invested most of it back into the company.

In early 1929 the world economy was shaky and Dad feared the stock market was about to crash. He tried to get Bruin and Harry to cash out, but they wanted to hold off until they could sell off some investments. When the market bottomed out on October 29, 1929, it was too late. Dad had to use the money he had left to pay off the million dollars in debt of his partners. After all, they were family.

Dad joined John Hancock Life Insurance Company and became one of its top salesmen. This meant my younger sister, Suzanne, and I had it better than a lot of kids during the Great Depression.

Ransom Jackson belted 103 home runs in the majors, including the last one hit by a Brooklyn Dodger. Ransom is shown here shaking hands with teammate Charlie Neal, left, after a two-run blast against the Chicago Cubs at Wrigley Field on August 28, 1956. Waiting to congratulate Ransom is Rube Walker, number ten. Ransom Jackson Collection.

One of Dad's good friends was Bill Dickey, a catcher for the great New York Yankee teams in the 1930s who was later inducted in the Hall of Fame. He had dinner at our house one night and gave me a stuffed deer head and a souvenir baseball that he along with Joe DiMaggio and other members of the 1939 Yankees had signed.

I put the deer's head on the wall in my bedroom, which had six windows and was at the back of the house. My cousin, Buddy Hill, lived with us for two years. At night he and I would lie in our beds and throw one dart each across the room at the deer's head. The winner was the one who came closest to a white spot on the side of the deer's neck; the loser had to open the windows at night and close them in the morning. Unfortunately, Buddy died during his freshman year at the University of Arkansas. I really missed throwing darts and the other fun things we did together.

The autographed baseball didn't fare any better than the deer. I took it outside and played catch with my friends. That ruined the signatures and rendered the ball worthless as a collector's item.

Baseball was just something to do with the kids in the neighborhood. There was a league for teenagers, but I didn't play in it long because I didn't know anybody.

The biggest summer attraction was a sock-ball league organized by Charlie Bennett, who lived across the street. The league had twelve two-man teams with names like the Baxter Street Boys, Elm Wood Racers, and Crystal Court Crusaders, which was my team.

Games were played in Charlie's backyard, a fenced-in area that measured about fifty feet by fifty feet. We played twice a week. Charlie posted the schedule two weeks in advance. If you didn't show up on time, your team had to forfeit the game.

The ball was two thick rolled-up socks with tape around them. The bat was a broomstick—the bigger and thicker, the better. Teams supplied their own ball and bat.

Baseball-type rules were adapted for the two-man teams. If a batter doubled, for example, his teammate had to score him with another hit or it was an out. They switched places on strikeouts. On defense, there was a fielder and a pitcher, who threw the sock ball underhanded.

Charlie didn't play so he could run a concession stand for fans who attended the games, sitting on benches or the branches of nearby trees.

He sold candy bars and cold, bottled soft drinks like Barq's Root Beer, a personal favorite, for a dime.

Charlie turned a profit at a time when few people had enough money to buy a television, computer, or mobile phone, even if they existed. Kids made up their own games for entertainment. Or we listened to the radio. Mom had dinner ready at six o'clock every night so we could follow the adventures of Buck Rogers and Hopalong Cassidy while we ate. Sometimes I tuned in to the radio broadcasts of the Little Rock Travelers, a minor-league team. The announcer orchestrated various gong sounds and crowd noises to re-create a lively account of the game based on bare information from Western Union ticker tape. It made me feel like I had a front-row seat at the ballpark.

There was no football program at my high school so I went out for the track and golf teams.

In track, I ran the 220-yard dash—at least that's what I practiced. At our opening track meet, however, the coach put me in the 440-yard race. It was my first time running that distance. At the halfway mark, I was in second, and then I faded to last. To this day, I can hear a voice in the stands yelling, "Come on and run!"

Golf was better, although I don't remember much about the team nor how I did.

My most vivid memories are of the City Golf Tournament in 1941 at one of Little Rock's public golf courses. The greens were sand and completely circular with the hole in the middle. There was a flat rake to make a path from your ball to the hole.

It was a two-day weekend tournament and, on arriving at the course, I learned I was in the championship flight. I was only fifteen years old.

There was a crowd in front of the clubhouse and around the first tee making a lot of noise. A God-like voice announced over a loudspeaker, "Quiet, please, championship flight." I almost wet my pants.

There was some comfort in knowing Dad was by my side. He was a scratch golfer who consistently shot in the seventies using only a three-iron, seven-iron, wedge, and putter.

On the first hole my opponent hit one straight over a hill between the woods on both sides of the fairway. I put the tee in the ground, placed the ball on it, and swung. The ball sliced over the trees to the left, disappearing over the hill. I walked off to a smattering of applause.

We were tied to start the sixteenth hole. I had won the previous hole, but my opponent teed off first anyway.

"It's illegal," Dad informed me. "If you call him on it, he'll lose the hole and you'll be one up going into the eighteenth."

I didn't want to win that way so I said nothing and lost on the final hole.

2

ADVENTURES WITH BUBBA

One reason I didn't play organized sports until college was I was having too much fun doing other things with my cousin, Bubba Beall, in Helena, Arkansas.

Every summer I spent about a month in Helena with the Beall family: Uncle Allein; his wife, Elizabeth (my mother's sister); and their three children, Cornelia, Upton, and Bubba, who was a year older than me.

Helena was right out of a Mark Twain novel—a Mississippi River town where the trees far outnumbered the eight thousand people that lived there in the 1930s and 1940s. Everybody talked real slow. Nobody walked fast because there wasn't much to do, unless you were a kid. Helena was the perfect place for me and Bubba to make our own adventures.

About four times a week, we'd get up in the morning, rub coal oil all over our legs and arms to ward off the chiggers, and take off into the woods, one of us carrying a hatchet and the other a hunting knife.

One day we saw a big bass in a stream about five feet wide and two feet deep. Bubba got in the water with a hunting knife; I was twenty yards upstream with a hatchet. Bubba tried catching the fish with his knife; I tried hitting it with my hatchet. The fish kept swimming back and forth between us. There were three little boys up on a levy watching us and they had no idea what we were doing. Finally, Bubba stuck the knife in the fish, holding it up like a trophy. It probably weighed four pounds. We gave the fish to the boys to take home.

Sometimes we'd gig frogs. Or we'd go down to the Mississippi River and shoot turtles with our .22 rifles. There were hundreds of turtles on logs about one hundred yards away. We missed more than we hit.

We always had a rifle with us in case we needed it.

Once we were fishing when our boat floated under some overhanging limbs. I looked up and saw a big snake hanging about ten feet above my head. I grabbed the rifle and, one-handed, shot the snake in the head.

Sometimes in the evening Uncle Allein took us to a bridge on the Long River a few miles outside town. There, we waited with our rifles for the gar to come to the surface. We shot the gar because they eat other fish and are not edible themselves.

We weren't always doing the shooting.

The Bealls lived on a hill near the main highway to West Helena. It was all trees the hundred yards from the house to a fifty-foot cliff overlooking the highway. Every now and then Bubba and I tried hitting cars passing below with balls of dirt. On one occasion we hit our target. The man slammed on his brakes, got out of his car with a rifle, and fired shots over our heads as we ran faster than we ever imagined. Needless to say, we never threw a dirt clod at a car again.

In the attic of his house, Uncle Allein had virtually every issue of *Life* magazine. I spent hours looking at them. There was also a series of books called Little Big Books that contained fictional stories. I read them all.

Uncle Allein was a seed broker and the funniest man I ever knew. There was one joke about picking cotton he could never finish telling because by the time he got to the punch line, his eyes were filled with tears from laughing so hard. It was more fun to listen to him laugh than it was to hear the end of the joke.

Helena had a country club where I played golf with Bubba and Uncle Allein. Neither of them was very good but they shared my love for the game.

Uncle Allein had a cabin on a nearby lake where we fished in the summer and hunted ducks in the winter. The ducks could usually be found in a forest that was completely under water.

Late in the afternoon we'd get in our boats and navigate through the forest until we came to an opening about the size of a baseball field. We put out decoys and then returned to the cabin where we had supper and slept on cots inside a screen porch. At night temperatures dropped below forty degrees Fahrenheit so we bundled up like mummies under a half dozen blankets.

In the morning, we got up at five o'clock, ate breakfast, jumped in the boats with our rifles and flashlights, and headed to our hunting spot about forty-five minutes away. There, we spread out along the side of the lake and waited for the ducks to fly over on their way from the rice fields to the Mississippi River. Usually we bagged eight to ten ducks and two or three big fat squirrels in the trees. One time the ducks came in for a landing on a frozen part of the lake, hit the ice, and kept on sliding. We broke out into laughter watching them.

Bubba's sister, Cornelia, had an infectious laugh just like her father. She married Jim Graham, a car salesman who was a pilot in the United States Air Force during World War II. They had four boys, one of them named Ransom after my dad.

One time they found an injured squirrel and nursed it back to health before turning it loose in their backyard. The squirrel liked to jump on Jim's shoulder as he was leaving for work.

My mother and Cornelia were like twins, although Mom was eighteen years older. In later years, they traveled together and played card games like Hand and Foot. Mom couldn't see very well because she had macular degeneration, and sometimes she put down the wrong cards. Rather than get upset, Mom and Cornelia laughed like it was one of the headlines in the hometown newspaper, the *Helena World*.

People bought the paper just to read headlines like: MAN FOUND DROWNED IN UNIDENTIFIED RIVER. There was another one about a woman "taking an operation in her stride."

The people of Helena had a knack for taking life in stride. That's what made the summers there so enjoyable and memorable.

We are shaped by our childhood experiences. Connecting them to specific things that happen to us as adults is difficult. Over the years, the words "natural" and "lazy" were frequently used to describe my performance on the baseball field. I was trying as hard as the next guy, but obviously it didn't appear that way. Was I laid back and easygoing because of the time I spent around the wonderful people of Helena?

I'll never know. But I do know the summer days I spent with Bubba were some of the best in my life.

3

ACCIDENTAL BIG LEAGUER

People frequently called me a natural athlete because golf, football, and baseball were easy for me. A better description is one used by a national sports publication: "accidental big leaguer."[1]

I made it to the majors through a series of highly unusual circumstances—accidents, if you will.

The lives of millions of Americans, including my family, were turned upside down by the stock market crash of 1929 and the Great Depression that followed. It happened again in 1941 on my sister Suzanne's twelfth birthday—December 7.

". . . a date which will live in infamy," President Franklin D. Roosevelt said in declaring war on Japan after its surprise attack on Pearl Harbor. World War II changed the world while shaping the rest of my life.

Just before hearing the news on the radio, I was playing football in front of my house with a friend, Jerry Barnes. We had a special game where we tried kicking the ball over each other's head with the street as a boundary.

I was two months shy of my sixteenth birthday—too young to go to war. Dad was nearly forty-two. He was considered too old when he volunteered to join the U.S. Navy, but he persisted by writing an undersecretary of the navy who was a classmate and friend at Princeton. Dad wound up running a flight school at a navy air base in Corpus Christi, Texas.

Mom remained in Little Rock until I graduated from high school and enrolled at the University of Arkansas in 1943. It wasn't long before I had to decide whether to volunteer for military service or take my chances on being drafted into the army.

I was always into airplanes. My dream was to join the navy air corps and become a pilot. Dad was in the air corps; he talked me out of it.

"There are three or four killed every week," Dad said. "It's not worth it."

He told me to apply for the navy's college training program, called V-12, so I could continue my education while preparing to be a commissioned officer. That's how I became a student at Texas Christian University in Fort Worth, Texas.

I was required to take twenty-one credit hours of classes a semester, including three navy courses and three regular courses such as physics, calculus, and English. If I flunked a class, I was gone, shipped out to sea. We were paid fifty dollars a month, and $18.75 of that went to buying a U.S. war bond.

We got up at 5:30 in the morning for exercises and attended classes until 3:30 in the afternoon.

Some of my friends played football, so I went out to see them practice.

"Why would anyone want to play football?" I wondered to myself.

The coach was Leo Robert "Dutch" Meyer. He walked up to me on the sidelines and introduced himself.

"Are you interested in playing football?" he asked.

"Coach Meyer, I'm in the navy and I don't really have the time."

"Well, if you're interested I'd certainly like to have you because we're a little bit short on men."

He only had thirty-something players because of the war.

I thought about it for a few days and then told Coach Meyer I'd give it a shot.

"What position did you play in high school?" he asked.

I had played football but only sandlot games on Sundays.

"I didn't play football in high school," I said.

"Go work out with the linemen."

I was six feet tall and weighed about 165 pounds. All of the linemen were bigger, several topping two hundred pounds. I was scared just looking at them.

I noticed the backfield guys weren't beating up on each other like the linemen; they were having a good time throwing the ball and joking around.

After practice I told Coach Meyer I'd rather be a halfback.

"All right, you can work out with them."

I was clueless about formations, blocking, tackling, and virtually every aspect of the game except kicking. I knew how to kick because of the game I played with my boyhood buddy, Jerry, in Little Rock. I was named the backup kicker.

The first-string kicker got hurt on the first play of the first game against the University of Kansas in Kansas City. I didn't have time to think about what I was doing. I just kicked. Seven times I punted the ball out of bounds inside the ten-yard line. One kick came within a half foot of the goal line. We won 7–0 and I was the most unlikely hero of the game.

I ended up playing both offense and defense, averaging about fifty-five minutes a game. By the end of the season, we had fifteen players, inspiring the nickname "Fifteen Fighting Frogs."

Another game I played with Jerry helped me as a running back. We marked out an area on a hill and then took turns trying to run the ball up the hill past each other. This went on until after dark. It didn't matter who won.

Despite being overmatched both in size and numbers, TCU won the Southwest Conference title to earn a spot in the 1945 Cotton Bowl against Oklahoma A&M and its all-America tailback, Bob Fenimore, college football's total offense leader.

Coach Meyer devised a trick kickoff return play to surprise the heavily favored Aggies. We practiced the play for two weeks and used it on a first-quarter kickoff after we fell behind 14–0.

The play called for the linemen up front to miss their blocks and run to the right sideline. There, they would form a running lane for me to follow into the end zone for a touchdown. This was to be set up by a lateral pass from our quarterback fielding the kickoff on the other side of the field. It looked better on paper than in the game, won 34–0 by the Aggies. The lateral was thrown behind me and by the time I scooped up the ball, an avalanche of tacklers buried me on the ten-yard line.

Ransom Jackson went from backup punter to running back for Texas Christian University in 1944, averaging about fifty-five minutes a game. He played in back-to-back Cotton Bowls in 1945–46, the first for the Horned Frogs and the second for the University of Texas. Ransom Jackson Collection.

Hoping I was as good at baseball as football, Coach Meyer invited me to try out for the baseball team he coached.

The only baseball I played growing up consisted of pickup games at a junior high school near my house in Little Rock. If four guys showed up, we played with four. If there were twenty-five, we made up a game for that number. Everything was seat of the pants.

"What position do you play?" Coach Meyer asked.

Dad played third base at Princeton, so I said third.

I surprised Coach Meyer and myself by leading the Southwest Conference with a .500 batting average.

In May 1945, the navy shut down its program at TCU and sent me to the University of Texas in Austin.

Dana X. Bible, the Texas football coach, saw me play at TCU and knew what I could do. He called and asked me to meet him at the stadium.

"Jackson," he said, "we've got a pretty good team and a nice quarterback coming in by the name of Bobby Layne. We'd like you to come out."

"I don't have time for football," I said.

Coach Bible wasn't very tall, but standing directly in front of me and looking into my eyes, he was a giant. "We need you," he said firmly.

It's not wise to reject a man named Bible. The season was almost a replay of the one at TCU.

We won the Southwest Conference championship with a 10–1 record and played in the 1946 Cotton Bowl. This time we won, outscoring Missouri 40–27. Layne, who went on to a Hall of Fame career in the National Football League, accounted for all forty points. He threw for two touchdowns, ran for three more, caught a fifty-yard bomb for another, and kicked four extra points. I became the first and only player in Cotton Bowl history to play in back-to-back bowls for different teams.

I ended up playing football one more year and two seasons of baseball, hitting .439 and .400 to win the league batting title three consecutive years.

Bibb Falk was the baseball coach at Texas for twenty-five years, winning consecutive national titles in 1949 and 1950 and twenty Southwest Conference championships. He played twelve seasons with the Chicago White Sox and Cleveland Indians after replacing Shoeless Joe

Jackson, the legendary outfielder banished from baseball for his role in fixing the 1919 World Series.

Falk was a punch hitter, spraying the ball all over the field during batting practice. It was the technique he used to hit .352 in 1924, third best in the American League behind Babe Ruth, the batting champion. For his career, Falk hit .314. I remember his batting stance and him riding the umpires the way he did in the majors to earn the nickname Jockey. He treated his players like big leaguers but made sure they didn't have big-league egos.

"That ball sure carries in this light air," he told a hitter who had just belted a grand slam in a regional tournament game in Denver, Colorado.[2]

When one of his stars hit a game-winning home run to the opposite field, he asked, "Are you ever going to learn to pull that pitch?"[3]

The only time Coach Falk complimented me was after I hit a ninth-inning homer to win a game. "Nice hit, son," he said.

On another occasion, he handed me a letter. Inside the envelope addressed to him was a three-by-five card with a handwritten message reading: "Can't you get a third baseman and get rid of that lousy Ransom Jackson?"

I received a letter around the same time from Chicago Cub scout Jimmy Payton wanting to know when I was getting out of college. I never dreamed of playing in the big leagues, so it was nice knowing somebody thought I could.

World War II ended with Japan's surrender in August 1945. The following June some five hundred navy students at Texas attended a meeting where it was explained we had three choices: (1) go into the regular navy; (2) go to sea for one year; (3) get out of the navy. I walked out of the auditorium along with 495 other guys.

I stayed on at Texas to play one more season of football and baseball and get a bachelor's degree in business.

In Helena, Arkansas, where my parents moved after Dad retired from the navy, I was a newly adopted son, the subject of the *Helena World* headlines everybody once laughed about: LOCAL YOUTH IS WRITING SPORTS HISTORY AT TEXAS UNIVERSITY.[4]

The story went into my football and baseball accomplishments at the University of Texas and Texas Christian University and how I scored eighteen points the first time I played in an intramural basketball game.

Ransom Jackson won three straight Southwest Conference batting titles, the first for Texas Christian University and the next two for the University of Texas. At Texas, he played for coach Bibb Falk, who replaced Shoeless Joe Jackson, the legendary Chicago White Sox outfielder banned from baseball for his role in fixing the 1919 World Series. Ransom Jackson Collection.

"Soccer looked interesting, so he gave it a try and starred in his first effort. The same went for water polo."[5]

Soccer was fun but I didn't like water polo. It was too much work.

The article concluded: "Local golfers who saw him in action on the Country Club course last summer can understand his ability to stand out in all branches of sport. He has the coordination of a natural athlete, and his lazy-appearing swing with the driver was consistently good for well over two hundred yards."[6]

In November 1989, I was named to the University of Texas's Longhorn Hall of Honor, a prestigious group of athletes that includes coaches Falk and Bible; pitcher Roger Clemens, a seven-time American League Cy Young Award winner; golf stars Ben Crenshaw and Tom Kite; and pro football greats Bobby Layne, Earl Campbell, and Tom Landry.

At the induction ceremony, Landry presented me with a plaque that reads: "Ransom (Randy) Jackson as certification of his selection for The Longhorn Hall of Honor in recognition of those qualities that brought credit and renown to The University of Texas at Austin."

I went to the University of Texas to be a navy officer and wound up in a sports hall of fame. Talk about an accident.

4

THE AMAZING BOBBY LAYNE

No athlete could stay out all night and play the same day like Bobby Layne. "I'm a fast sleeper" is how he explained his unusual ability to hoot with the owls and soar with the eagles.

Now, I've heard about the exploits of Babe Ruth and Mickey Mantle. But they were outfielders and could take a breather every now and then. Bobby was in the middle of the action as a pitcher in baseball and quarterback on the football field.

Even when he was on his back physically, Bobby was on his toes mentally.

Playing for the Detroit Lions in the National Football League, he was sacked for a loss by Art Donovan, a 270-pound defensive tackle for the Baltimore Colts. Donovan was sprawled on top of Layne, virtually nose-to-nose because Bobby never wore a helmet with a face mask.

"Bobby," Donovan said, "we're going to get drunk smelling your breath. You must've had a helluva night last night."

"I had a few at halftime," Bobby quipped.[1]

I'm one of the few who played alongside Bobby in both football and baseball at the University of Texas. We were teammates for two seasons each in football (1945 and 1946) and baseball (1946 and 1947).

Bobby's idea of exercise and conditioning was going out on Friday nights before a game and throwing back a couple of six-packs of beer. The next day (or same day, if he rolled in Saturday morning) he could throw the ball wherever he wanted, his passes as easy to catch as a

Bobby Layne was almost a one-man show for the University of Texas football team, throwing and running for touchdowns as well as kicking field goals and extra points. About the only thing he didn't do was punt. Here, Ransom Jackson shows the form that made him one of the top punters in the Southwest Conference. Ransom Jackson Collection.

feather pillow. In three seasons at Texas, he passed for a school record 3,145 yards, completing more than 50 percent of his throws.

He could pass, run, and kick, and he did all three in the 1946 Cotton Bowl where the final score really was Bobby Layne 40, Missouri 27. He completed eleven of twelve passes, two for touchdowns. He ran for three more and kicked four extra points.

A "Statue of Liberty" play that didn't result in a touchdown was one of the most exciting in the game. Bobby dropped back as if he was going to pass. I ran behind him, taking the ball out of his hand and throwing it to Hub Bechtol, our all-America end, for a fifty-five-yard gain. The play is difficult to execute so it's rarely used. But there was hardly anything Bobby couldn't do.

When Bobby walked out to the pitcher's mound, it was usually "game over" for the other team.

In one game he pitched a no-hitter, striking out sixteen. Batting right-handed, he belted a double and then, hitting left-handed, got another double and single.

He threw almost straight overhand with a big, sweeping curveball that had batters swinging at balls bouncing in front of the plate. He was dominating. Proof of that is a perfect 28–0 won-loss record against Southwest Conference opponents and 39–7 mark overall. His two no-hitters in 1946 are still a conference record.

To beat Bobby, it took another two-sport sensation with big-league talent.

In the finals of the 1947 Western NCAA baseball playoffs, Bobby lost to the University of California and Jackie Jensen, a pitcher for the Golden Bears as well as an all-America football player. Jensen went on to become a star outfielder for the Boston Red Sox, winning the American League's Most Valuable Player Award in 1957.

Bobby took a shot at pro baseball in 1948, appearing in twelve games for the Lubbock Hubbers of the Class C West Texas–New Mexico League. He won more than he lost (6–5), but his earned run average of 7.29 more closely resembled the yards he gained per carry in college. Pros didn't swing at Bobby's curveballs in the dirt.

That's just as well. Bobby's forte was football. He became a National Football League legend, prompting *Sports Illustrated* to call him "The toughest quarterback who ever lived."[2]

For me, Bobby always will be the most amazing quarterback who ever lived.

5

FROM CONROE TO THE CUBS

The war was over. Televisions and air conditioners were not yet household products. People had time and money on their hands. Going to the ballpark on a hot, humid night to see a baseball game was the most popular thing to do in many Texas towns the summer of 1947.

It was the heyday for baseball in Texas. The closest major-league teams were the Cardinals and Browns in St. Louis, but there were thirty-four minor-league teams in the state and dozens more semipro teams.

Conroe, Texas, located forty miles north of Houston, was organizing a team of "College Joes"—the best players from Texas colleges.

I had just won my third straight Southwest Conference (SWC) batting title at the University of Texas so I was offered $400 a month to play for the team. And what a team it was—seven of the players made the 1947 all-SWC team. The Conroe Wildcats didn't lose a game in capturing the state semipro championship.

At the time, Conroe had a population of 4,624. Of that number, an average of eight hundred, roughly 17 percent of the population, attended the games. Once, 1,700 fans showed up.

One major-league team, the Browns, even approached one of the Wildcat owners, Ty Cobb, about Conroe joining one of the lower classified minor leagues. "We aren't in this to make a job outta it," Cobb said. "We just like to mess around with the boys. We get as mucha kick out of this club as they do."[1]

Cobb managed the Wildcats on the field as well.

"He isn't the IMMORTAL Ty Cobb, but he is darned nearly immortal in Texas semipro circles," reported a sportswriter for the *Victoria Advocate*.[2]

"I like to work with these college boys," Cobb said. "They are easy to manage, and then I like to spoof myself into believing that I help them get through school and make good players."[3]

Cobb was wiry little guy but a big-league character.

He was about to get into a fight one game in Houston when I picked him up from behind so he wouldn't get thrown out. He turned around and hit me in the face for stopping him. It was fun!

We played three or four games a week and went fishing on days off.

The state semipro tournament in Waco lasted three weeks. As the top-ranked team, our games started at eight o'clock at night and usually ended around 10:30.

We couldn't afford to stay overnight in a motel, so we drove three and a half hours back to Conroe—four of us in a car. Midway we stopped at a huge watermelon patch. One guy served as a lookout, another thumped the melons to see if they were ripe, and two carried them back to the car. When the trunk was full, we continued on to Conroe, arriving around three in the morning. We went straight to an icehouse and scratched our initials on the melons. After each game, typically played in ninety-degree heat, we returned to enjoy the ice-cold watermelons with our initials on them.

Semipro baseball in the oil fields of east Texas in the late 1940s was serious business. A lot of money changed hands between the fans.

After soundly beating one team, we got a call from one of its players asking us to be imposters for them against another team we also had whipped badly. They had a grudge to settle and offered us fifty dollars each to wear their uniforms and play on their behalf in this highly secret scheme.

We jumped in four cars and drove to a gas station outside the town where the game was to take place. There we were given silk softball uniforms with this team's name on them. They barely fit.

We paraded into the ballpark a little embarrassed and almost certain the tight-fitting silk uniforms would blow our cover. The other team recognized us immediately. But they didn't seem to care, probably because they now had an undefeated pitcher recently recruited from Louisiana.

We batted first. I doubled with two runners on; the next guy homered. We scored seven runs in the first inning on our way to a 14–4 victory. The pitcher from Louisiana was mystified; the fans that lost big bets were seething.

Each of us picked up a bat, walked slowly to the cars, and then sped off to the gas station to return the silk uniforms to the happy guy who instigated the moneymaking deal.

In September 1947, Chicago Cubs scout Jimmy Payton arranged for me to fly with my father to Chicago for a tryout at Wrigley Field.

It was a rigorous test, batting against Russ Meyer, a pitcher the traveling Cubs left home to recover from a sore throwing arm. He was a fiery competitor who eventually won ninety-three games in the majors, earning the nickname "Mad Monk." Angry over pitches called balls by an umpire, he once heaved a resin bag thirty feet in the air, and it came down on his head.

Meyer threw fastballs, curves, screwballs, everything except the resin bag. It was one of those days everything clicked. Line drives were flying all over the place, a couple out of the park.

Afterwards, the Cubs offered me a two-year contract at $6,000 a year. I thought big leaguers made double or triple that, but it was still a lot of money in those days. Besides, I was assured a place on the Cubs' forty-man roster and a chance to make the team the following spring.

Payton, the scout, was seeing stars. "The kid is just a natural athlete," he told a Chicago sportswriter, adding: "You watch, he'll be at third base for the Cubs by 1949. And it wouldn't surprise me if he made it next year."[4]

In three months, I went from playing semipro baseball in Conroe to signing a major-league contract with the Cubs. In my wildest dreams, that never happened.

6

TRAINING WITH THE GOATS

The Wrigley family owned the Chicago Cubs and Catalina Island, twenty-six miles across the sea from Los Angeles, so Catalina was the Cubs' spring training home when I joined the team in February 1948.

To get there, the Cubs sent me a letter with three tickets. One was to travel by air from Little Rock to Chicago, and the other two were for the train from Chicago to Los Angeles and the steamship from L.A. to Catalina.

The train was late arriving in downtown L.A. By the time my taxi reached the port of San Pedro twenty-five miles away, the SS *Catalina* was steaming out of the harbor. It was too far to swim and there wasn't another boat leaving for the island until the next day.

"How can I get to Catalina?" I asked a guy who looked like he might know.

"There's a seaplane down the road that takes off in fifteen minutes."

We flew over the SS *Catalina* on our way to the island, arriving thirty minutes before it docked in Avalon, the island's main town.

I walked several blocks to the Hotel St. Catherine and found Bob Lewis, the team's roly-poly traveling secretary. He assigned me a room and grudgingly reimbursed me for my traveling expenses after making a smart remark about the cost of the cab rides and the seaplane flight.

This was my introduction to Catalina, a rocky island twenty-two miles long, eight miles across at its widest point, and a world apart from my home state of Arkansas.

The Cubs trained there nearly every spring from 1921 to 1951.

Ronald "Dutch" Reagan, a future president of the United States, filed reports on the Cubs from Catalina as a sports announcer for a radio station in Des Moines, Iowa.

Norma Jean Dougherty lived in Avalon with her U.S. Merchant Marine husband before she became famous as Marilyn Monroe.

Kevin "Chuck" Connors and Dee Fondy, both first basemen acquired from the Brooklyn Dodgers, were competing for a starting assignment with the Cubs in 1951 at Catalina's version of Wrigley Field.

I played against Chuck in the International League so when the Cubs asked about him, I gave two thumbs up. Fondy won the starting job, relegating Chuck to the Cubs' Pacific Coast League affiliate in Los Angeles, where he eventually became an actor and star of *The Rifleman*, a popular television series from 1958 to 1963.

Chuck played in only sixty-six games for the Cubs, batting .239. Still, my recommendation of Chuck to the Cubs was better than Jack Brickhouse, the team's play-by-play announcer, advising him to go by the name Kevin if he wanted to make it big in show business. "The name Chuck Connors is too common," Brickhouse said. "It won't catch on."[1]

Chuck used his time on Catalina to prepare for his acting career. Wherever there was an audience of two or more interested people, Chuck delivered a dramatic recitation of the classic baseball poem "Casey at the Bat."

William Wrigley Jr. and his son, Philip (P.K.), architects of the Wrigley chewing gum empire, envisioned Catalina as a casino resort and playground for rapidly growing L.A. The presence of the Cubs on the island for a month every spring generated countless wire-service photos showing players frolicking against a backdrop of swaying palms and sun-splashed mountains. Piggybacking on this free national publicity were ads beckoning Cub fans freezing in the Midwest: THE CUBS ARE HERE! WHY DON'T YOU COME, TOO?[2]

Catalina was a fun place. There was more wildlife than nightlife, and Avalon was so small you could see almost everything in town by wandering around for fifteen minutes. But there was fishing and a nine-hole golf course where we could play a round of golf after baseball practice.

The first week of spring training was limited to exercising, primarily running, because league rules didn't allow batting and fielding practice until the first day of March.

In 1950 a minor-league pitcher named Lee Holloman showed up at Catalina with his wife, Nan, and three-year-old son, Gary. This was unusual because there was nothing for families to do on the island. Nan solved the problem by working out with the team. Whatever exercises we did on the field, she did the same ones on the other side of a fence as we watched.

Lee proved to be as resourceful as his wife. Returned to the minors at the end of spring training, he reemerged from obscurity as Bobo Holloman in 1953 with the St. Louis Browns to pitch a no-hitter. "Bobo's No-No," sportswriters called it.

"Big Bobo was born to be a hinterlands drummer," outspoken Browns owner Bill Veeck said. "He could outtalk me, outpester and outcon me. Unfortunately, he could not outpitch me. In spring training, he was hit harder trying to get the batters out than our batting practice pitchers who were trying to let them hit."[3]

Bobo got bombed in four relief appearances prior to his no-hitter.

"So Bobo reached into his bag of tricks and went to work on us," Veeck said.[4]

"You haven't given Big Bobo any chance," he told Browns manager Marty Marion. "Big Bobo isn't a relief pitcher, he's a starter. Big Bobo can pitch better than half the guys you've got starting."[5]

Bobo tried his charm and humor on Cubs manager Frank Frisch, a cantankerous soul other players avoided like the plague.

"That meathead wouldn't let me pitch to show what I had," Bobo complained. "I kept asking him to lemme pitch. Finally he said to shut up or he'd ship me out. The next day I was on my way."[6]

Nan echoed this in a book she wrote about her husband: "If Frisch could have shown a little more patience and confidence in Bobo's bold confidence, this big right-hander from Georgia, who lived baseball, might have been a winner for the Cubs."[7]

Frisch was like a drill sergeant at a military boot camp. He had us hike all day in the mountains, using the winding, uneven paths made by the goats. We did this for five straight days. Everybody got shin splints and a few suffered cactus needle wounds. We were lucky not to be attacked by wild boars or trampled by bison, descendants from a herd left over from a movie shoot in the 1920s.

Exhibition games were held at L.A.'s Wrigley Field, a clone of the one in Chicago. Each day about half of the forty-man roster would fly to L.A. for the game and back to Catalina for the night.

The airport was located on top of a mountain. The runway was barely long enough for our plane. On takeoff, the plane dropped about a thousand feet toward the ocean before leveling off. It was scary. Nobody wanted to fly to L.A. to play a game. If your name was on the list posted daily, you started feeling sick to your stomach. If you were not on the list, you were happy because you could work out and go play golf.

The highlight of spring training was an all-day fiesta at Rancho Escondido, P.K. Wrigley's mountain retreat where he raised Arabian horses and had a tack room with a $25,000 saddle and other riding equipment. We went by boat to a seal colony and then by shuttle bus to the ranch.

Mountain goats captured alive by Wrigley and his cowboys were the targets of roping contests among the players. After the rodeo, there was a barbecue featuring beef and goat meat and Connors taking center stage to do his thing with Casey and the Mudville Nine. It was a fun time in a fun place and even more fun to think about all these years later.

7

FIELD OF DREAMS

Long before there was a movie about a field of dreams in Iowa, there was a sensational new car on display at Pioneer Park in Des Moines, Iowa, that had every player on the Des Moines team dreaming about it.

The vehicle was hailed as "the first completely new car in fifty years."[1] The player selected the most popular by fans would drive off in the cutting-edge car at the end of the 1948 season, courtesy of a Des Moines radio station. Fan clubs did most of the voting so the players enthusiastically attended meetings of their respective fans.

The Des Moines Bruins were the Chicago Cubs' team in the Class A Western League. For most of us, playing in Chicago was well down the road, if we even made it that far. The chance to win a dream car made Des Moines the place to be.

I was happy to be there and playing for "Smiling" Stan Hack, the greatest third baseman in Cubs history until he retired the year before.

The Bruins were training in Macon, Georgia, when I joined the team and got introduced to quirky playing conditions common in the lower minors at the time.

The field was laid out strangely. There was no fence in the outfield, but there were big telephone poles with lights. The poles weren't far from home plate so outfielders had to run beyond the lights into the dark chasing long fly balls. They carried a ball in their pocket so when they emerged from the darkness, they had one in their hand to show the umpire that the ball was caught for an out.

Stan Hack, left, was a four-time All-Star at third base in his sixteen years with the Chicago Cubs. Ransom Jackson, right, credits Hack with teaching him how to play third base, beginning in 1948 when he was manager of the Des Moines Bruins. Hack also managed Ransom at Springfield, Massachusetts, in the International League in 1950 and again in 1954–55 with the Cubs in the majors. Ransom Jackson Collection.

There was nothing weird about Pioneer Park in Des Moines. It was one year old, almost as new as the dream car that was a huge incentive for the players to go all out for the fans.

Early on, I had trouble throwing the ball to first base. Many times fans caught my errant tosses instead of the first baseman. "Random Ransom!" some fans heckled.

Hack shadowed me throughout infield practice before games, looking for clues that could improve my balance and throwing accuracy. I wound up with thirty-three errors but had more putouts, assists, and double plays than any third baseman in the league.

My bat turned most of the catcalls to cheers.

I was hit in the head by a pitched ball one night, and the very next evening I singled twice and had one of my best games on defense.

"Listen," said one of my teammates, "when they tell you to keep your eye on the ball, they don't mean for you to take it that literally."

I rubbed my puffy, purple left cheek and joked, "And just when I was getting rid of that shiner I got in fielding practice."

The Bruins won the pennant. I had a .322 batting average, six home runs, and seventy-six runs batted in to make the Western League All-Star team and finish second in the voting for the team's Most Valuable Player.

The contest for the most popular Bruin came down to me and first baseman Russ Kerns, who batted .275 with twenty-one homers. The last day of the season it was announced that Russ won by twenty votes.

They rolled the car onto the field and Russ got into it for the first and last time.

The car we all dreamed about driving was the 1948 Tucker sedan, envisioned by its creator, Preston Tucker, as the car of the future. Advertisements for the Tucker promised it was "the car you have been waiting for."[2]

Russ is still waiting. The '48 Tucker never made it to market, the fifty production cars scattered over time among collectors and museums. One of them is on display at the Smithsonian National Museum of American History in Washington, D.C., a vivid reminder of my own field of dreams.

8

ALMOST THERE

In 1949, my second year as a pro, I made it to Wrigley Field. But it wasn't the one in Chicago. It was the look-alike ballpark by the same name in Los Angeles, a popular location for filming movies like *The Winning Team*, with an actor named Ronald Reagan playing Grover Cleveland Alexander, the alcoholic pitcher who won 373 games.

I made a cameo appearance for the Los Angeles Angels of the Pacific Coast League, playing fourteen games prior to being optioned to the Oklahoma City Indians in the Texas League, at Class AA—one step closer in the baseball hierarchy to the majors.

Oklahoma City was affiliated with the Cleveland Indians, so I was an outsider. It was a veteran team by minor-league standards, the average age around twenty-eight. I didn't know any of the players and they knew nothing about me. None of this seemed to matter at the time.

Grant Dunlap, the team's right fielder, went on to be a highly successful baseball coach at Occidental College and write a novel, *Kill the Umpire*, focusing on the Texas League in 1949. The central character is "Handsome" Ransome Burton, a slick-fielding second baseman for the San Antonio Missions and the only college graduate on the team. "The guys get on me about it all the time," Ransome is quoted as saying.[1]

In 1949 there were few players with college degrees in pro baseball, but I had no idea it was the source of any resentment until Dunlap told me after publication of the book in 1998.

Dunlap's novel mixes fact with fiction, describing the Oklahoma City Indians as "the best hitting team in the league" and first baseman Herb

At age twenty-three, Ransom Jackson was a kid compared to the old pros who made up the rest of the Oklahoma City Indians infield in 1949. Pictured, left to right, are Ransom; Frankie Zak, twenty-seven; George Scharein, thirty-four; Mickey Burnett, thirty; and Herb Conyers, twenty-eight. Except for Burnett, all of them played in the majors. Ransom Jackson Collection.

Conyers, nicknamed "Ole Abe" because he looked like Abe Lincoln, as the best of the bunch. "Pitchers were serious and aged appreciably when they faced him," Dunlap wrote.[2]

Conyers led the league in batting average (.355), hits (214), and doubles (fifty-two). Altogether four players hit .300 or better and batted in more than a hundred runs. Conyers and Dunlap made it to the majors along with several other Oklahoma City players, including pitcher George Zuverink, a sixteen-game winner who eventually became a top reliever for the Baltimore Orioles.

The Indians were a good team in a good league. I was also closer to where my parents were living in Helena, Arkansas. They could see me play more often.

Dad arrived in Oklahoma City the morning after I got hit in the head a second time in as many seasons. He was at a service station when he heard an Indians fan say, "I sure hate to see that Ransom get out of the lineup."

"That's my name and that's my son you're talking about," Dad said. "What'd he do, make a lot of errors?"[3]

The fan explained I was struck in the temple but not seriously injured.

Dad was at the game that night and saw me dive into the stands to catch a pop fly and belt a triple and grand-slam homer. Once again I responded to a beaning with a few hits of my own.

I was one of the hottest hitters in the league, but midseason the Cubs paid $35,000 for Bill Serena, a husky, power-hitting third baseman for the Dallas Eagles, another Texas League team. In a Class C league two years earlier, Serena blasted seventy home runs. Thirteen of them came in fourteen playoff games. This set the stage for a third-base battle between me and Bill that would continue in the majors.

Serena remained with Dallas where he finished the season with a .281 batting average, twenty-eight homers, and 110 runs batted in. I ended up with similar numbers: a .298 average, nineteen home runs, and 109 RBIs. Combined with my statistics in L.A. to begin the year, I had twenty-one homers and 115 RBIs and missed the magic .300 mark by one percentage point.

The two of us were the subject of a survey of Texas League managers by John Cronley, a sports columnist for the *Daily Oklahoman*. "If they had to have a big league third-baseman for immediate duty they'd grab Serena," Cronley wrote, "but over the long route they would choose Jackson as the boy most likely to blossom into the big league stardom."[4]

We were about to find out if the managers were right.

9

NEW KID IN TOWN

One month into my first year in the majors, Chicago Cub manager Frank Frisch compared me to one of baseball's all-time great hitters, Rogers "Rajah" Hornsby. A *Sporting News* headline proclaimed: KID JACKSON LOOKS LIKE RAJAH AS ROOKIE.[1]

I was beginning my third year in pro ball. I didn't know much about Hornsby or most of the players on the other teams. I had never stepped foot in a big-league ballpark except the day of my Cub tryout at Wrigley Field.

There wasn't a hat size big enough for my head. The Big Show was the Big Easy. I was on my way to the Hall of Fame. Move over, Rogers Hornsby.

First, I had to move aside Bill Serena, the third baseman the Cubs had invested $35,000 in the year before. That was a lot of money in those days—nearly six times my salary. I could do the math. The Cub brass had to start Serena at third.

I watched the first five games of the 1950 season from the bench. Frisch was more comfortable with Serena at third base because he had a rifle for a throwing arm and was less likely to do something defensively that might trigger one of Frisch's many temper tantrums.

Serena didn't get a hit until the fifth game. He was 1-for-19 when Frisch decided to give me a shot.

I singled twice, doubled, and tripled in my first two starts. "The extra base wallops crashed off the distant walls despite a stiff in-blowing wind," Edgar Munzel reported in the *Chicago Sun-Times*.[2]

I went hitless the next game, so Serena was back in the lineup because of his "superior defensive play."[3]

This set up a series of strange events against the Brooklyn Dodgers at Wrigley Field that got Frisch thrown out of the game and me put in it as a defensive replacement for Serena.

In the top of the eighth inning, a Dodger runner was called out at third when Serena tagged him—and then, safe when he dropped the ball. Bill was charged with his second error of the game.

"Frisch argued vigorously that the fumble didn't occur until after the play," Munzel wrote in the *Sun-Times*. "But he lost. And he got the bounce on top of it."[4]

By the time Frankie reached the clubhouse and turned on the radio, Gil Hodges had thumped a three-run homer to give the Dodgers a 6–3 lead. Frisch was listening in the bottom of the ninth inning when Hank Sauer answered for the Cubs with a three-run, game-tying shot and I smashed a homer into the left-field bleachers to lead off the tenth.

"It was the crowning touch in a display of bulldog spirit such as the Dodgers, including Branch Rickey himself, who sat in a ringside box, hadn't encountered in a Cub team in several years," Munzel observed, adding it was vindication for me.[5]

"He's a great competitor—that loose, relaxed style of his reminds me for all the world of Rogers Hornsby when the Raj was breaking in," Frisch gushed after he missed seeing my first big-league homer.[6]

"He could develop into one of the great hitters in the game," Frisch told Munzel.[7]

It was heady stuff, although Frisch acknowledged that comparing me with Rajah was "a bit preposterous."[8]

Baseball is a game where you can quickly go from the outhouse to the penthouse and back. That's what happened after my walk-off homer against the Dodgers. I had one hit in my next twenty-six at bats. I struck out three times in one game.

On May 31, twenty-six days after I was banner headline news in Chicago newspapers, the Cubs sent me back to the minors, this time to Springfield, Massachusetts, in the International League.

I wasn't surprised or disappointed. In fact, Springfield was the place to be as I was reunited with "Smiling" Stan Hack, my first manager in pro ball. My defensive play improved, and I regained the hitting stroke that reminded Frisch of the legendary Rajah.

A sliding Ransom Jackson is tagged out at home plate by Brooklyn Dodgers catch-er Roy Campanella. Ransom's first big-league homer was against the Dodgers, a game-winning shot in the tenth inning of a game at Wrigley Field May 5, 1950. Ransom Jackson Collection.

At Springfield, I hit .318 with twenty home runs and was named the team's Most Valuable Player and the International League's Rookie of the Year to earn another ticket to the Big Show.

The Cubs were in Boston to play the Braves. There were about two weeks left in the season and the Braves were close behind the first-place Philadelphia Phillies.

"I don't care who wins the pennant," Frisch growled at Boston sportswriters, "just so the Cubs win a ball game."

Frank was in a bad mood. The Cubs had lost eleven out of their last twelve games, including four straight.

I was notified that morning in Springfield to take a train to Boston, so I arrived just in time to dress for the game and take batting practice.

"Want to play tonight?" Frank asked.

It was a frigid night—too cold to sit on the bench or the stands that were almost empty. I didn't want to make Frank mad, either.

"Sure, I'm ready."

Pitching for the Braves was Vern Bickford. He was one win short of becoming a twenty-game winner, the magic mark for pitchers.

I was the leadoff hitter. When I stepped into the batter's box to begin the game, I could hear people talking in the stands. The crowd of 3,392 was the smallest for a night game in Braves Field history. I hit what appeared to be a home run until a high wind knocked it down and back onto the field for an out.

Bickford was cruising along with a shutout when I faced him in the top of the eighth, a runner on first. I fouled off the first pitch. I was looking for a curveball and got it. According to the *Boston Herald*, I "swung from the heels on the next one" as "the ball disappeared between the top of the double-decked fence and the bottom of the score-board."[9]

Kid Jackson was no Rajah, but he was back in Chicago to stay.

10

BIG NOSE SAM, THE BASEBALL FAN

Sam Cufari was just another fan except for a rather large nose.

I noticed Sam soon after I joined the Springfield Cubs seven weeks into the 1950 season. Springfield was the Chicago Cubs' Class AAA affiliate in the International League, a step up from the Texas League where I played for Oklahoma City the year before.

Sam attended every Springfield game, sitting behind the Cub dugout.

"Who is that guy?" I asked one of my new teammates.

"You don't know who that is?"

"I wouldn't have asked if I knew."

"That's Big Nose Sam Cufari, head of the Mafia here in Springfield."

The technology didn't exist to Google Big Nose Sam. All I had to go on is what I was told and eventually experienced.

Most fans in Springfield left immediately after a game. Sam lingered around to talk baseball with the players. After several friendly conversations, he asked, "Would you like to play golf at my country club?"

"Sure," I said, not seeing any harm in playing a round of golf with my roommate and one of our loyal fans.

At 7:30 the morning we were to play, a big limousine pulled up outside our apartment. A big guy with a bent nose knocked on the door. He escorted us to the country club.

Inside on a counter, there were slot machines filled with golf balls.

"You need some golf balls?" Sam asked.

We fed fifty-cent coins into the slots for our golf balls and then went into the locker room and got dressed, slipping on golf shoes supplied by Sam. When we returned after playing eighteen holes, the clubhouse was cleared so we could feast on the Italian delicacies spread across a large table. We did this twice.

Sam had a nice restaurant in downtown Springfield that I ate at occasionally. I heard that there was gambling in another area of the building, but I never went there.

"You can borrow my car anytime you want," Sam said.

"I really don't need one, but thanks for offering."

I didn't hear from Sam again until late in 1951 when I was back in the majors with the Cubs. We had finished our second doubleheader in as many days against the New York Giants. I had already eaten dinner and was resting in my hotel room when the telephone rang around 9:30.

"Randy, this is Sam Cufari!"

"Sam, how you doing? Haven't heard from you in a while."

"I'm in New York and we're having dinner. Come on down and see me."

"I'm awfully tired, Sam. I just finished two doubleheaders and I've got another tomorrow."

"Come on down," he persisted.

I didn't want to upset someone like Sam so I headed to the restaurant, a short walk from the hotel.

I was met at the door and ushered to a back room with a long table. There were four couples sitting on each side with Sam at the end. He waved to me. "Come on down."

I walked past these guys who might as well have had M-A-F-I-A written on their foreheads. It was a scene right out of *The Sopranos* television series.

I sat down next to Sam.

"Have you eaten?"

"Yes, I have."

Sam loved baseball, so that's what we talked about while he ate.

"Have you ever had this before?" Sam asked, pointing at the calamari he was obviously enjoying.

"No," I said.

"Have a bite!"

"I don't think so, Sam."

"Have a bite!"

It was an offer I couldn't refuse, so I took a bite. It was like biting into a Goodyear tire.

Around eleven o'clock, I got up from my chair. "Sam," I said, "I really enjoyed seeing and talking with you. If you want to go to the game tomorrow, I'll leave you some passes."

"I have some other things to do, but thanks anyway," he said.

As I left, I spoke to everybody, stopped, and waved goodbye. "See you around," I said.

That was the last I saw of Sam. I read about him in the newspapers, so I know a lot of other people didn't consider him to be as nice as I did. Over six decades he was arrested and charged with numerous Mafia-related crimes, but he never spent a day in prison.

I don't remember much about golfing with Sam except I'm pretty sure he won. I enjoyed our conversations and knowing that if I ever had problems with any bad guys, I could turn to Big Nose Sam.

Part 2

The Big Leagues

11

WHO'S ON THIRD?

The big question in 1951 as the Chicago Cubs began spring training on Catalina Island was: Who's on third?

The season also had a touch of Bud Abbott and Lou Costello's famous comedy routine, "Who's on First?"

When Phil Cavarretta, a longtime Cub first baseman, replaced Frank Frisch as manager in July, he bluntly said the team needed a first baseman, two outfielders, and three catchers. After he'd been on the job awhile, he declared, "We're aching down the middle."[1]

About the only position he left out was third base where the competition between me and Bill Serena for the starter's job continued. Bill won the first round in 1950 and posted a batting average of .239 with seventeen homers and sixty-one runs batted in.

"Serena's only chance of restoring himself to his status of last season lies in a miraculous improvement in the gentle art of annihilating National League pitchers," John Hoffman of the *Chicago Sun-Times* reported during spring training.[2]

The Cub brass still had visions of Bill bashing home runs like he did in 1947 at Lubbock, Texas, in the Class C West Texas–New Mexico League. He belted fifty-seven during the regular season and thirteen more in the playoffs.

"How did you hit seventy home runs?" Bill was asked.

"The accordion did it," he said, noting that it helped him relax. "It lifted my morale. It made me confident."[3]

I played the piano, but it wasn't music Frisch wanted to hear. He wanted me to holler and leap on fumbled ground balls.

"What did your football coach tell you to do when there was a loose ball?" Frank asked.

"Fall on it."

"That's what I want you to do."

A *Chicago Daily News* headline declared: LACK OF SPIRIT RETARDS RANSOM.[4]

"I know what's bothering the skipper," the story quotes a player who is referring to the dour Frisch. "He's trying to figure out the best way to put a firecracker under Jackson."[5]

The article goes on to say that "Jackson can't miss baseball greatness—if only he can acquire some dash and spirit."[6]

I finished the exhibition season batting .362, but that didn't keep Serena from opening the season at third base.

In early May Bill was swinging one of the hottest bats on the team with a .333 batting average when his left wrist was struck and broken by a pitched ball. He was out for the year. And I was in.

Things didn't go well at first.

"Jackson was batting a trivial .200 and the Cubs' board of strategy was beginning to sob audibly," Hoffman wrote in the *Sun-Times*. "Serena would be back at third base the moment his wrist could be mended."[7]

Suddenly, I went on a home run binge—four in three games. "From an almost easy out," Hoffman wrote, "the transition brought out the beast in the laconic twenty-five-year-old rookie."[8]

By July even Frisch was saying nice things about my defense: "He's been making the darndest plays, one after another."[9]

I was hitting .270 with twelve home runs and was considered a strong candidate for National League Rookie of the Year.

"What's wrong with Chicago having both rookies of the year . . . with Orestes Minoso as the American League winner and Ransom Jackson of the Cubs getting the palm in the National League?" asked *Chicago Daily News* columnist John P. Carmichael.[10]

That was wishful thinking as the New York Giants had a twenty-year-old rookie who would become the greatest defensive center fielder to ever play the game—Willie Mays.

Mays won the award, but our numbers were almost identical. Willie out-homered me twenty to sixteen while my batting average of .275 was one point higher and I had seventy-six runs batted in to his sixty-eight. Surprisingly, I had twice as many stolen bases—fourteen to Willie's seven.

I was feeling pretty good about the future, especially after reading what several National League managers said about me in a newspaper story.

"Jackson's going to be one of the best third basemen in the league," said Marty Marion of the St. Louis Cardinals. "He can do everything."[11]

"He's got a great pair of hands," added Tommy Holmes of the Boston Braves.[12]

"The boy looks like a real good hitter," said Billy Meyer of the Pittsburgh Pirates. "Good power and speed."[13]

In December there was a news report that the Braves were trying to make a deal for me but the Cubs wanted in return first baseman Earl Torgeson, who was coming off a highly productive season—twenty-four homers and ninety-two RBIs. The Cubs still needed to answer their own who's on first question.

The Abbott and Costello classic is about a team in St. Louis, although it could've easily been about the Cubs in 1951.

Abbott: "I'm not asking you, I'm telling you: Who is on first."

Costello: "I'm asking you, who's on first?"

Abbott: "That's the man's name."

Costello: "That's whose name?"[14]

I answered the question of who's on third with a solid first year, and it was widely known that other teams in the league wanted me. Surely, the Cubs would reward me with a healthy increase over the major-league minimum I was making.

There was no free agency nor agents at the time. You went one-on-one against general managers who knew you had nowhere to go. Take it or leave it. You're lucky to be in the big leagues.

The Cubs offered me a disappointing $2,500 raise, bumping my salary up to $9,000.

I wrote Wid Matthews, director of player personnel, citing my Willie Mays–type stats and the league-leading number of putouts and assists I had on defense. He was on record as saying I was one of only two Cub players the Brooklyn Dodgers had interest in, so I added a footnote about my value in the marketplace.

"There was one other team that wanted you and all they offered was a broken bat, a caved-in catcher's mask and an old ball," Wid replied. "The best thing for you to do is to get your things together and get down to spring training and try to make the team."

I signed that contract and ran as fast as I could to the post office to mail it back to the Cubs.

12

THE POWER OF CHOCOLATE DONUTS

Baseball players are the most superstitious of athletes. Almost every hitter and pitcher has a routine that he follows religiously.

Hitters put their feet in the same position in the batter's box, tap the bat the same number of times and in the same place, and fidget with their batting gloves the same way after every pitch. Pitchers are just as busy, often touching their mouth, cap, and uniform in quick succession with the fingers of their throwing hand. When they leave the field at the end of an inning, many pitchers make sure they step over the chalk line.

If a pitcher has a no-hitter after the fifth inning, he can usually be found sitting alone in the corner of the dugout. Nobody will say anything. There's a long-held belief that talking about a no-hitter in progress will cause it to end.

There are superstitions around things as simple as sticking a bat in the bat rack. When I played, there was a number on the end of most bats. Mine was K-55. Some guys insisted the number be parallel to the ground.

Harry Walker, the only player to win a National League batting title while playing for two teams during the same season, was called "Harry the Hat" because he was constantly taking his cap off and putting it back on at the plate. Harry credited the fidgeting with helping him hit .363 overall for the St. Louis Cardinals and Philadelphia Phillies in 1947. "When I step away from the batter's box, fix my hat and my hair, I relax my muscles," he said, "and maybe I get the pitcher and catcher upset."[1]

Joe DiMaggio, the New York Yankees great, always reached down and touched second base as he jogged out to his position in center field.

Several players were obsessive about coming to the ballpark at exactly the same time every day. They ate and drank the same things before every game. When they got dressed, they made sure they put their uniforms, socks, and shoes on the same way. One guy went on a hitting streak and wouldn't let anybody wash his socks. Fortunately, I was upwind from his clubhouse locker.

There were players who had a special spot on the bench where they sat. Tobacco chewers always sat near a fresh supply of pouches provided by the folks at Beech-Nut.

I wasn't particularly superstitious, but I had a daily routine I followed. When I was going badly, I tried different things to get back on track.

Going into a game on May 16, 1951, against the Brooklyn Dodgers at Wrigley Field, I had no home runs, and my batting average was under .200. That morning for breakfast I ate two chocolate donuts.

Carl Erskine, a rising young star, was pitching for the Dodgers. I came up in the first inning with a runner on. I swung and *wham!* The ball sailed into the bleachers in left-center field. Against a different pitcher the next inning, I slammed a three-run homer into the same area. The four runs batted in were one more than my output for the season.

"Two chocolate donuts, two home runs," I said to myself. "That's it! The secret is chocolate donuts."

I had two chocolate donuts the following day and belted a first-inning homer plus two singles.

My batting slump was over, and Chicago sportswriters took note. One of them attributed my success to a tip from a coach to move my elbows farther away from my body. "With my elbows close to my body, I couldn't swing naturally," I was quoted as saying. "I was missing pitches right down my alley—balls I should have knocked out of the park."

The chocolate donuts were my secret weapon, and I didn't want to talk about them. Nobody would've believed me anyway.

I got three more hits the next game—two singles and a two-run homer.

Chocolate donuts fueled a home run hitting binge by Ransom Jackson in 1951. In three games, he slammed four homers, scored nine runs, and batted in eleven more. In this photo taken in 1955, Chicago Cub teammate Gene Baker, number thirty-seven, is about to shake Ransom's hand after he beat the Cincinnati Redlegs with a two-run blast unaided by donuts. Ransom Jackson Collection.

In three games, I had four home runs, scored nine runs, batted in eleven more, and, with eight hits in fourteen times at bat, raised my batting average seventy-nine percentage points, from .182 to .261. The *Chicago Tribune* published a big photo of me taking batting practice. The headline read: HOME RUN POSE HELD BY RANSOM.[2]

I continued eating chocolate donuts, but I didn't hit any more homers the rest of the month. Of course, the donuts didn't have anything to do with my home run rampage. But they sure did taste good.

13

BATTING BEHIND THE MAYOR

After thirty years on Catalina Island, the Chicago Cubs moved their spring training camp to Mesa, Arizona, in 1952. It was warmer in Mesa and there was a lot more to do off the field. You could soothe your aches and pains in one of the natural hot springs nearby or go to a greyhound racing track and bet on the dogs. There was one named Randy Jackson, so I put my money on him. He placed eighth in a field of eight.

I didn't do much better with the bat. In fact, 1952 was a dog of a year. Hitting slumps come and go, but this one never went away. My batting average dropped from .275 to .232; home runs from sixteen to nine; and RBIs from seventy-six to thirty-four.

These numbers can be chalked off to the sophomore jinx that has left many rookie stars wondering if they were a one-year flash. Or they can be blamed on Hank Sauer, the Cubs' good ol' country boy who hit the ball a country mile in 1952 to lead the National League with 121 RBIs and tie Pittsburgh slugger Ralph Kiner for most home runs with thirty-seven. It was a performance worthy of the league's Most Valuable Player Award and the nickname "Mayor of Wrigley Field."

"When I think of Hank Sauer, I think of home runs and chewing tobacco, but not necessarily in that order," said longtime Cub announcer Jack Brickhouse.[1]

Sauer played left field, and when he trotted out there after hitting a home run, bleacher fans showed their appreciation by showering him with packs of Beech-Nut chewing tobacco. The packs that didn't fit into his pocket, he stored in the vines of ivy covering the brick wall.

Sauer batted fourth in the lineup; I hit fifth. He would hit a home run, and then the pitcher would knock *me* down in retaliation. I never could figure that out. I hadn't done anything.

One game, for example, Sauer slammed a three-run shot over Wrigley Field's left-field wall off George "Red" Munger of the St. Louis Cardinals. Munger plunked me on the next pitch. According to the records, this was the only time I was hit by a pitched ball all year. That's deceiving because I always had bruises from landing on the ground to avoid fastballs aimed at my head. As poorly as I was hitting, pitchers should've been looking out for me instead of throwing at me.

Some hitters are thinkers—they keep a mental or written log on each pitcher so they have a better idea of what to expect. It makes sense because a starting pitcher typically goes over the opposing lineup with his catcher and defense before a game. Think and prepare. I wasn't a

Ransom Jackson was a primary target for National League pitchers in 1952 as he often batted behind Hank Sauer, the so-called Mayor of Wrigley Field and the league's Most Valuable Player with thirty-seven homers and 121 runs batted in. Here, Ransom hits the dirt after being plunked in the shoulder in a game against the New York Giants in 1954. Ransom Jackson Collection.

thinker and I never prepared for a game in any sport—baseball, football, or golf.

Nobody ever sat me down and said, "You've got to be thinking about these things."

I never had a manager or coach say, "This is how you hit the ball to right field."

Or: "This is how you do it."

Rogers Hornsby was the Cubs' hitting instructor for a while. He had nearly three thousand hits and a career .358 batting average. Hornsby often was standing a few feet from me at the batting cage, but he never said one word about hitting. He seemed more interested in getting the game over with so he could go to the racetrack and watch some real thoroughbreds.

Harry "The Hat" Walker, a former National League batting champion, briefly played for the Cubs in 1949. He went on to become one of baseball's most respected hitting instructors.

"The secret is waiting," Harry said. "Stroke the ball inside, inside out. The only kind of guy who should try to pull the ball is a guy who can hit you forty homers a year."[2]

Harry hit only ten in eleven big-league seasons.

At spring training during batting practice at Los Angeles's Wrigley Field, we goaded Harry, a left-handed hitter, into trying to hit a ball into the right-field bleachers. They were so close I could almost throw the ball into the seats from home plate.

He'd swing hard and spray line drives all over right field.

"Harry, anybody can do this," we said, laughing.

But Harry couldn't do it.

In retrospect, I should've been pestering Harry for batting tips instead of teasing him about not hitting homers.

I wound up teaching myself to be a zone hitter. If the ball was in my zone, I took a cut. It was as basic as you can get—see the ball and hit it.

I didn't realize it at the time, but my problems in 1952 likely were caused by not thinking enough about the adjustments opposing pitchers were making. They discovered my weaknesses and were taking advantage of them. If I was going to survive in the majors, I needed to make some changes of my own.

I started in November when I married Ruth Fowler, a flight attendant from Athens, Georgia, I had met on a trip during the season.

We moved to Lawton, Oklahoma, to help my parents run a laundry and dry cleaning business they had acquired earlier in the year. It was one of Lawton's leading laundries located near Fort Sill, home of the United States Army Field Artillery School. With five thousand soldiers year-round and groups of two thousand more coming in for about a month of reserve duty throughout the summer, the business thrived for a while. Then the army quit sending reservists to the base.

After working in the laundry during the off-season, I was looking forward to playing baseball again—even if it meant batting behind the "Mayor of Wrigley Field."

14

HOT TIME IN THE GARDEN

In baseball terminology, third base is the hot corner and the outfield is the garden.

Of the 846 major league games I played on defense, 844 were at the hot corner where I was directly in the line of fire on shots off the bat of Henry Aaron, Willie Mays, Ralph Kiner, and other powerful right-handed hitters. Twice I found myself in the garden—left field. The first time in Cincinnati was hotter than any game I spent at the hot corner.

A game on a sizzling summer day at Cincinnati's Crosley Field, the Redlegs' ballpark for nearly sixty years, is what I imagine it would feel like playing in Death Valley.

Making matters worse, the Chicago Cubs' traveling secretary booked us a downtown Cincinnati hotel with no air-conditioning during the 1951–52 seasons. At night after games we'd take the sheets, put them under the cold water faucet in the bathroom, wring them out, run and throw them on the bed, and then jump in to try and get some sleep.

At Crosley Field, we tried dipping towels in mint-flavored water and wrapping them around our neck and head. The towels smelled good, but they didn't have much of a cooling effect. Someone suggested using cabbage leaves to stay cool. So we dipped leaves in ice water, squeezed out the water, placed them inside our caps, and went out to the field. They didn't do any good, either, so we got rid of them before the game started.

All we could do during one Sunday afternoon doubleheader in 1952 was grin and bear it.

The official temperature was ninety-seven degrees Fahrenheit. In the rooftop press box, it was 104. Down on the playing field, it was hot as hell.

After the first game, Hank Sauer, the Cubs' star left fielder, was so drained by the heat, he was in a daze. Even at his best, Hank could look lost on defense. So this was cause for concern.

Cub manager Phil Cavarretta came to me before the second game.

"Jackson," he said, "Sauer can't make it. You're playing left field."

I had never played the outfield and said so.

"It doesn't make any difference. You're playing left field."

Now, left field at Crosley was a challenge for even the most experienced outfielders. The wall was 328 feet from home plate. Starting about twenty feet out from the wall, the ground went up four feet at a fifteen-degree angle until it was level with the wall.

Babe Ruth, playing for the Boston Braves, had an embarrassing encounter with this incline, called "The Terrace," just before he quit baseball in 1935. Going back to catch a fly ball, Babe tripped and fell flat on his face.

I found out quickly what it was like to be in Babe's shoes.

The first ball hit to me was a high fly that I ran backward to try and catch. Running up a hill backward is not advisable. I fell on my butt, the ball dropping next to me untouched.

Finally, I realized the thing to do was to play a little bit up on the slope and run down instead of up.

I didn't play left field again until my final season with the Cubs in 1959. The game against the Dodgers was at night in the Los Angeles Memorial Coliseum. There was a forty-foot-high wire mesh net screen behind me but no hill. I pretended like I was playing a deep third base and made sure I didn't try climbing the screen. So my last visit to the garden ended a lot better than my first.

15

FIRE AND MONEY

One way to end a season-long slump is to get married.

Not only did I hit for average (.285) and power (nineteen home runs) in 1953, Chicago sportswriters reported I was no longer "droopy or unhappy" and now showing "new-found exuberance" and "new hustle" as a newlywed. It was interesting reading. How much of it was true and had anything to do with my marriage to Ruth Fowler in late 1952 is debatable.

One writer attributed my improved hitting to playing less golf. "Anybody who shoots in the low 70s can't be thinking exclusively about baseball," Ed Burns wrote in the *Sporting News*.[1]

Throughout my career with the Cubs I had to put up with comments about my "lugubrious mien and languorous approach"[2] to the game. I wasn't exactly sure what that meant, but I knew it wasn't flattering.

One wag suggested that "Smiling" Stan Hack, my manager for two years in the minors, taught me how to play third base but *not* how to smile.

According to the critics, I was too mechanical and lacked fire. A *Chicago Daily News* article in 1951 quoted a scout as saying, "If someone can set off a spark in him, he's likely to burn up the league."[3]

This was a common theme, starting with Frank Frisch, my first Cub manager.

Frisch was a track star and all-America halfback at Fordham University where he earned the nickname "Fordham Flash." He went directly from college to the majors with the New York Giants where he was described as a whirling dervish for his aggressiveness. He was player-manager for the St. Louis Cardinals in the 1930s when they were called the "Gashouse Gang" because of their scrappy, hell-bent style of play.

When Frisch was fired by the Cubs amidst criticism from some players, he fumed, "Real ballplayers never talk, they just play ball. You won't find any .320 hitters or twenty-game winners among those gripers."[4]

On succeeding Frisch as manager, Phil Cavarretta picked up the torch: "Ransom Jackson could make us a great third-baseman if I could find some way to build a fire under him, make him play the way he knows how all the time."[5]

In trying to build that fire, Cavarretta invoked the name of Bill Serena, my competition at third. "What a great player Jackson would be if he just had Serena's fire."[6]

Cavarretta was a serious, no-nonsense guy. He said what he thought and meant what he said. As a player, he'd run through a brick wall to get a ball. I've run into enough of life's "brick walls" to know the wall always wins.

Even Frisch came to terms with my style of play, asking: "How do you make a kid like that holler and hustle if it just isn't his nature?"[7]

I'm simply not a rah-rah or fire-and-brimstone kind of guy. You've got to be calm and relaxed to hit a fastball traveling ninety-plus miles per hour or react quickly enough on defense to turn a sure hit into an out. I tried as hard as any player who made a lot of noise. My playing style was consistent with my approach to life in general. What matters most is the end result. Getting a timely hit or stolen base and making a clutch defensive play is far more important than having smoke coming out your ears.

Frisch also was right when he said: "Real ballplayers never talk, they just play ball."[8]

The only way to silence my detractors was to keep my mouth shut and just play ball. I had to regain the edge on pitchers who caught up with me in 1952.

My comeback started on Opening Day with a two-run, game-winning double against Cincinnati's Ken Raffensberger, a longtime nemesis with twenty-seven career wins over the Cubs.

I hit over .400 through most of April, slumped in May, and then got it going again in June when Ralph Kiner joined the Cubs after a blockbuster ten-player trade with the Pittsburgh Pirates. Kiner was a big name coming to a team of no-names, with the exception of Hank Sauer.

Kiner was the greatest power hitter in baseball at the time with seven straight National League home run titles. He blasted thirty-seven in 1952 to share the crown with Sauer. Now they were teammates, and I didn't have to worry about one of Kiner's line drives ripping off my head at third base.

The downside of the deal was on defense. If Frank Frisch thought I ran like a turtle, he would've likened Kiner and Sauer to a couple of sloths. Sauer was slightly faster so he moved to right field, leaving behind the packs of chewing tobacco he stashed in the ivy on the left-field wall.

In between Kiner and Sauer was Frank Baumholtz. Frank wasn't exactly a speed demon and he wasn't a center fielder. But he had to play there and do his best to cover the entire outfield. As hard as Frank

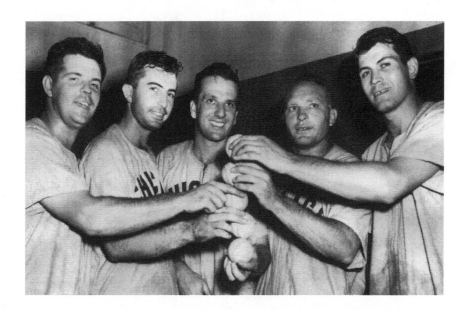

Ransom Jackson established himself as a star in 1953, batting .285 with nineteen homers. One of those homers came in a doubleheader against the New York Giants on June 8, 1953, in which the Chicago Cub players pictured clouted six out of the park. Left to right: Eddie Miksis; Jackson; Ralph Kiner, who hit two; Clyde McCullough; and Dee Fondy. Ransom Jackson Collection.

huffed and puffed, he couldn't reach a lot of balls that should've been caught.

I was hitting .300 with thirteen homers in July when Ralph did a column, Kiner's Liners, for a Chicago newspaper saying I belonged on the National League All-Star team. "I had always suspected that Jackson might be quite a hitter but until I had the opportunity to observe him every day I had no idea the power he had in his swing," he wrote.

I wanted to give Ralph a hug for this line: "His baseball swing, like his golf swing, is a masterpiece of timing, and he gets his power from his wrists. He snaps the bat into the ball at the last split second to get the maximum distance."[9]

"Take that, Ed Burns," I thought to myself, recalling the sportswriter who questioned my commitment to baseball because I was a good golfer.

Recently, I found a story in a scrapbook quoting Paul Richards, manager of the Chicago White Sox.

Asked why an ex–football player like Jackson "didn't bring more pepper" to baseball, Richards replied: "As a halfback Jackson learned to relax between plays, an athletic gift. He relaxes when he's not executing a play in baseball and has got a reputation as being droopy. But he's a fine player and could make a lot more money probably if he did a lot of snorting and hollering when the ball is not in his vicinity."[10]

More than sixty years have passed since Richards made that statement. I realize now that snorting and hollering was the way to show more fire and make more money.

16

MAKING WAVES ON WAVELAND

Standing at home plate watching a home run soar out of sight was a death wish in the 1950s. Pitchers like Sal "The Barber" Maglie needed little provocation to give batters a close shave with a fastball.

If ever I wanted to admire a home run, it was one that flew over the left-field bleachers and Waveland Avenue, bouncing off the third floor of an apartment building overlooking Wrigley Field. They didn't have a way to accurately measure home run distances in those days, so all I know is that it was my longest home run and a sign of the good things to come in 1954 and 1955.

I was named to the National League All-Star team both years, belting nineteen home runs in 1954 to match my previous best and a career high of twenty-one the next year. My wife, Ruth, gave birth to our first son, Randy, in July 1954, and Chuck the following year.

The Chicago Cubs welcomed a new shortstop named Ernie Banks, the team's first African American. Ernie and second baseman Gene Baker joined the Cubs near the end of the 1953 season to become the first black double-play combination in the majors. My only thought when they arrived was: "They must be good players or they wouldn't be here."

It didn't take long to realize that Ernie was going to be great. He was a natural hitter who with just a flick of his wrists could generate amazing power. On defense, he had great range and a strong throwing arm. Gene actually was a better shortstop than Ernie, but he was six years older and more experienced, making the move to second base easier for him.

Leading the Cubs was Stan Hack, my manager-mentor in the minors at Des Moines and Springfield. His signature smile and easygoing style was a refreshing change from his predecessor, the stoic Phil Cavarretta.

But some things never changed.

I was hitting .600 (6-for-10) through the first two games only to read in a Chicago newspaper that I was "phlegmatic" and "goaded to anger" by Hack's initial decision to open the 1954 season with Bill Serena at third base. The story's headline was: SERENA'S BID FOR JOB LIGHTS FIRE UNDER JACKSON.[1]

The arrival of Ernie Banks, far right, in late 1953 added even more power to a Chicago Cub lineup that included Ransom Jackson, far left, and Hank Sauer. In 1954, their first full season together, Jackson and Banks each hit nineteen homers while Sauer smashed forty-one. Ransom Jackson Collection.

"The phlegmatic third baseman also has been doing a bang-up job on defense," another writer reported in an article titled HACK'S HUNCH PAYS OFF.[2]

The shot heard on Waveland Avenue came in the third game when I got four more hits and the Cubs scored twenty-three runs. In the sixth game I had four singles and a home run—5-for-5—to raise my batting average to .615. I received a Western Union telegram reading: THAT'S BETTER. SHOULD HAVE HAD MORE THAN ONE HOMER THOUGH BATTING AVERAGE CLOSE TO MINE—DAD.

A sports columnist in Lawton, Oklahoma, quoted Dad as saying, "I hit .600 on an amateur team one summer and I told Randy he should do the same thing. I guess the boy is taking my advice."[3]

I went into the 1954 All-Star Game July 13 in Cleveland with a .310 batting average, sixteen homers, and fifty-five runs batted in for the first half of the season. I was the only Cub named to the team.

"Jackson has done such a superb job both afield and at the plate that it was considered a grave miscarriage of justice in many sectors that he wasn't voted to the starting lineup in baseball's annual mid-summer classic," Edgar Munzel observed in the *Sporting News*.[4]

I had no qualms with the fans selecting Ray Jablonski of the St. Louis Cardinals to start at third base. It was a real field of dreams to be part of a game involving fourteen future Hall of Famers—Willie Mays, Stan Musial, Jackie Robinson, Duke Snider, Roy Campanella, Red Schoendienst, Robin Roberts, Warren Spahn, Mickey Mantle, Ted Williams, Yogi Berra, Larry Doby, Bob Lemon, and Whitey Ford.

I grounded out my first time up in the eighth and batted again in the ninth with the National League trailing, 11–9, one runner on and two outs. A home run tied the score. I popped out to end the game.

In an interview with a Cincinnati sportswriter before the All-Star break, I was asked how it felt having such a good year. "Really good," I said, "and I hope the other guys can get going and have good years, too."

The story made my comment sound like I was the only guy on the team producing and nobody else wanted to win. Cub owner Philip K. Wrigley called and told me to apologize publicly for what I supposedly said. "I didn't say what the reporter wrote," I explained.

I never got the apology I requested from the writer, and I refused to take back something I didn't say in the first place.

Perennial All-Stars Ralph Kiner, far left, and Stan Musial, center, discuss Ransom
Jackson's chances of making the team prior to a game in 1954 at Wrigley Field.
Jackson was selected to the National League All-Star team in 1954 and 1955.
Ransom Jackson Collection.

Randy was born at four o'clock the morning of July 16. Despite
being up all night, I played that afternoon against the Pittsburgh Pirates. Twice I had to be awakened and told to get ready to bat. I had
one embarrassing moment in the field when a ground ball was hit to me
at third with a runner on second. Thinking it was a force play and the
last out of the inning, I stepped on the bag and flipped the ball toward
the pitcher's mound. Everybody started screaming and hollering to pick
up the ball. Somehow I got two hits, stole a base, batted in a run, and
made only the one mental mistake on defense.

Dad sent me another telegram July 22 after I hit two homers against
the New York Giants to give me nineteen for the season: THOSE
HOME RUNS, THAT'S MY BOY. GO! GO! GO!—DAD.

Unfortunately the home runs stopped. I didn't hit another one, and my batting average dropped to a season-ending .273.

The cause of the slump was an infected right hand that put me in the hospital for three days and out of the lineup for nearly a month. The hand remained sensitive and weak the rest of the year.

I got off to another sizzling start in 1955 with four homers in the first five games. Three of them came in successive at bats, including two in a game against the Cardinals when Banks and Dee Fondy also connected twice. We hit three straight to tie a major-league record.

The next game I had to quit midway when I noticed swelling in the same hand that was previously infected. This time I was out two weeks.

I was one of four Cubs to participate in the 1955 All-Star Game in Milwaukee. Banks started at shortstop, "Toothpick" Sam Jones pitched,

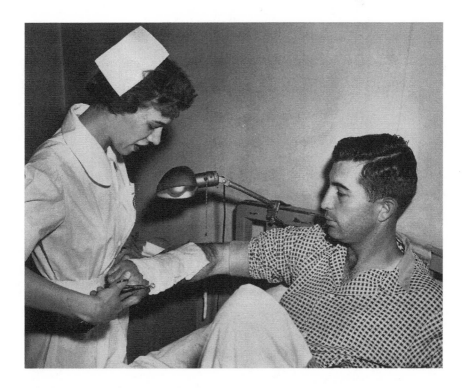

Pitchers couldn't stop Ransom Jackson in 1954 and 1955, but a hand infection hampered his performance both years. One of the infections was the result of a spider bite. Ransom Jackson Collection.

Baker pinch-hit, and I entered the game at third base in the top of the seventh inning with the National League trailing 5–0.

We scored twice in the bottom of the seventh. In the eighth, I drove in a run with a single off Ford and scored the tying tally to send the game into extra innings. In the bottom of the twelfth, another substitute hit a walk-off home run to win the game 6–5. As one writer said of the homer, "A ball game never is over until Stan the Man is out."

Playing in back-to-back All-Star Games was the highlight of my Cub career.

A once-promising season that saw the Cubs begin June in second place ended in disappointment as the Cubs faded in the second half to finish sixth, twenty-six games behind the pennant-winning Brooklyn Dodgers.

I didn't know it at the time, but my next stop was Brooklyn. I'd be wearing a Dodger uniform the next time I saw my favorite apartment on Waveland Avenue.

17

ONE OF A KIND

Sam Jones was different. He always had a toothpick in his mouth, possibly explaining the sad, forlorn look on his face and the mumbling when he spoke. When Sam could throw his amazing curveball for strikes, he had opposing batters mumbling to themselves.

Sam was the first African American to throw a no-hitter in the major leagues—a 4–0 gem against the Pittsburgh Pirates at Wrigley Field on May 12, 1955. Like Sam, the no-hitter was different.

Sam was in his first season with the Chicago Cubs, joining the team in the trade that sent Ralph Kiner to the Cleveland Indians. He already had three victories, one more than he had in his big-league career up to that point. He had the stuff needed to be a big winner. The only question was whether or not he could get the ball over the plate.

Through eight innings, Sam walked only three. He was three outs away from throwing the first no-hitter at Wrigley Field in thirty-eight years.

There were far more empty seats than the 2,918 fans in the ballpark, but there was plenty of tension as Sam walked the first three batters in the ninth. The bases were loaded with the Pirates' best hitters to follow—Dick Groat, Roberto Clemente, and Frank Thomas. A home run not only spoiled the no-hitter, it tied the game.

I hurried to the pitcher's mound from third base. The rest of the infield followed—shortstop Ernie Banks, second baseman Gene Baker, and first baseman Dee Fondy. We were huddled around Sam and catcher Clyde McCullough when manager Stan Hack popped out of the dugout. We looked the other way.

Stan was looking for help. It was obvious what he was thinking: "Do I leave him in or take him out?"

I didn't want any part of removing Sam from a no-hit game. "It's all yours, buddy," I thought to myself. "That's what managers are for."

"How do you feel?" Stan asked Sam.

"Fine."

Stan turned to Clyde. "How's his stuff?"

"Okay. Leave him in the game."

That's what Stan wanted to hear.

"Settle down," he said to Sam. "Just get the ball over and make them hit it."

All of us were relieved, especially Hy Cohen, a rookie right-hander who was warming up in the bullpen in case Stan changed pitchers. "I was about to shit in my pants," Hy admitted later.

Sam got the ball over like Stan said except nobody hit it.

Three fast curves mesmerized Groat, who didn't swing at any of them.

Clemente, in his rookie year, fouled off two pitches before striking out.

Thomas, the Pirates' biggest threat to hit a home run, was next. In the fourth inning, he ripped a line drive to third that I caught for an out. I was braced for another hard smash. I didn't want to blow Sam's no-hitter.

The first pitch to Thomas was a strike, the second a ball. He missed a high curve and then took a called third strike.

It has to be the most dramatic ending to a no-hitter.

"I went further with Jones than I ordinarily would have," Hack said later. "But had the fourth Pirate reached base, he would have been out of there."[1]

The game gained legendary status over time. Cub play-by-play announcer Jack Brickhouse said he met twenty thousand fans who claimed to be at the game—almost seven times more than the number actually there.

The first question Brickhouse's sidekick, Harry Creighton, asked Jones immediately after the no-hitter was: "Sam, how's the family?"[2]

"That had to be one of the greatest lines in sports broadcasting history," Brickhouse said.[3]

Harry can be excused for not knowing what to say because he had never seen a Cub pitcher throw a no-hitter at Wrigley Field. A couple of days later he presented Sam with a gold toothpick from Cub owner Philip K. Wrigley. Sam also got a $1,000 bonus.

Sam went on to lose twenty games and lead the National League in walks and strikeouts. Four years later he won twenty-one games for the San Francisco Giants. Altogether, he had 102 wins in the majors. The biggest and most incredible of all was a one-of-a-kind no-hitter.

18

A HISTORY-MAKING WALK

Barry Bonds was intentionally walked a record 688 times by pitchers who didn't want to see how far he could hit the ball. I received eleven intentional walks in my career. One of them made history.

I didn't know this as I trotted to first base at Wrigley Field in the first inning of a game against the St. Louis Cardinals April 12, 1955. It wasn't my first intentional walk. But as I later found out, the four pitches Brooks Lawrence purposely threw wide to put me on first base were different.

Check the lifetime statistics for Babe Ruth, Lou Gehrig, and Joe DiMaggio, and you'll find that no intentional base on balls (IBB) is listed for them. Why?

They played before 1955 when baseball statisticians decided it was time to officially document and track IBBs.

Runners were on second and third when I faced Lawrence in the bottom of the first inning. There was one out. First base was open, so I was given a free pass to load the bases and set up a possible double play with the next batter, Ernie Banks. He walked to force in a run, and Dee Fondy followed with a three-run double.

The IBB is listed in the box score, but nobody bothered to mention that it was the first *recorded* IBB in National League history.

I didn't know I was involved in any kind of first until many years later.

I was talking with Loran Smith, a newspaper columnist and radio announcer based in Athens, Georgia, where I've lived since 1956.

"You're the first one to do something," Loran said one day.

"What was it?" I asked.

"I can't remember," Loran said.

This went on for years.

"Do you remember what I was the first one to do?"

"No, I can't remember," was always the reply.

A few more years passed before the mystery was solved by an inquiring sportswriter who said, "Do you know that you're the first recorded intentional walk in the National League?"

"Yeah, and they can't find the recording," I thought to myself.

I was skeptical, pointing out that there were a bunch of intentional walks before I got to the majors in 1950.

"Yeah, but they weren't recording all these intentional walks. You're the first in the National League."

I mentioned this to the guy who started it all.

"Loran," I said, "was it the first recorded intentional walk in the National League that you were trying to remember?"

"Yeah, that's it!" he said.

In the American League, Joe Astroth of the Kansas City Athletics was intentionally walked in the second inning of a game played the same day in Kansas City. Since my walk came one inning earlier in a game that started around the same time, it's possible I edged Joe by a few minutes for bragging rights in both leagues.

Admittedly, an intentional walk is no big deal. All a batter does is stand there like a tree while the pitcher lobs four balls to the catcher. But playing for the Cubs, there weren't many chances to be first. You take a history-making walk when you can get it.

19

WASTING AWAY IN WRIGLEYVILLE

Ernie "Mr. Cub" Banks once described the Chicago Cubs as a team that "played together and lived apart." The Dodgers, he noted, "were close, they all lived in Brooklyn, they were all good friends."[1]

The Cubs of the 1950s were mainly a bunch of castoffs brought in willy-nilly with no plan other than keeping the team payroll as low as possible.

"In those days, we had one-a-comin', one-a-playin' and one-a-goin'," said Bob Speake, a rookie sensation with the Cubs in 1955 when he belted ten home runs in the month of May before cooling off and winding up on the bench the latter part of the season.[2]

The Cubs were particularly fond of ex-Dodgers, hoping their winning ways rubbed off on other players. Obviously they didn't. The turnover was constant. There was no camaraderie. There was no team.

When the Cubs played the Dodgers in Brooklyn, for example, I felt we were starting the game behind 1–0. The Dodgers' togetherness off the field made them even better on it because they fed off their wildly enthusiastic fans at Ebbets Field. They also knew how to win and they expected to win. That's the difference between a habitual winner and loser. If they play every day, the habitual winner will prevail most of the time.

From TCU to Texas in college football and Des Moines to Oklahoma City to Springfield in the minors, I always played on winning teams.

The Cubs had a losing record each of my twelve years as a pro with the exception of 1952 when they broke even with seventy-seven wins and losses. Four times they ended up last in the National League. If you're content to be on a last-place team, you're not much of a player. You want to be a winner.

The Cubs' problems on the field in the 1950s can be traced to the apathy of owner Philip K. Wrigley at the top of the organization to the front-office bungling of Wid Matthews, the club's personnel director from 1950 through 1956.

Other than the barbecue P.K. hosted at his ranch on Catalina Island when the Cubs trained there, the players rarely saw him. I met P.K. only once.

In 1948 the United States reinstated the military draft. Men between the ages of eighteen and twenty-five were required to register for service. I was playing for the Cubs in Des Moines so I signed up there.

By 1951 the U.S. was fully engaged in the Korean conflict, and major-league rosters were particularly vulnerable. "Military background was placed even ahead of the traditional 'throws right—bats left' notation," one writer said of Matthews's appraisal process.

I was enjoying my first full year with the Cubs when I got a letter in August 1951 from my draft board in Des Moines saying I was being drafted into the United States Army as a buck private. I wrote back that I was a full lieutenant in the U.S. Navy Reserve. The army's response was essentially, "Who cares? We're drafting you anyway."

I met with P.K. in his office to explain the situation. He arranged for his son-in-law to escort me to the Great Lakes Naval Station where we were to meet a friend who was an admiral there. The admiral wasn't in town so we talked to his chief of staff. He reviewed my papers and then wrote a letter to my draft board, saying I was in the naval reserve and couldn't be touched. "Don't worry, son," he said, "if worse comes to worst, we'll draft you back in the navy and you can play third base for Great Lakes."

Several months later I got another letter from the Des Moines draft board, this one apologizing for the mistake and wishing me and the Cubs good luck the rest of the year. It's great to know people in high places.

P.K. kept me out of the army but, in general, he remained in the background, letting Matthews do everything else.

"I do not infallibly state that Wid had a knack for doing the wrong thing," wrote David Condon, a *Chicago Tribune* columnist. "Let me say that had Owner Wrigley sent him for a package of gum, tho, Wid probably would have returned with Beechnut."[3]

Matthews played pro baseball for twelve years, mostly in the minors, before going to work for Branch Rickey, then business manager of the St. Louis Cardinals. He became one of Rickey's most trusted scouts and advisors in building championship teams for the Cardinals and Dodgers.

In 1949 he scouted Willie Mays for the Dodgers after star catcher Roy Campanella recommended his signing. Wid reported that Willie couldn't hit a curveball. "Who ever heard of any seventeen-year-old hitting a curveball?" a puzzled Campy asked.[4]

Matthews joined the Cubs in 1950. After losing twenty-five games more than they won, he placed every player on the waiver list. Four went through unclaimed. Outfielder Andy Pafko was claimed by nine teams; eight were interested in outfielder Hank Sauer, shortstop Roy Smalley, and pitcher Bob Rush; and seven wanted me along with pitchers Johnny Schmitz and Frank Hiller. "We had a seventh place ballclub," Wid explained, "but we discovered our players hold the respect of rivals."[5]

Matthews admitted that the Cubs were fundamentally unsound.

"Our first step is to hold kindergarten classes," he said. "As fans must realize, we have quite a few players on our roster who were brought to the majors too soon. As a result, they have outstanding weaknesses. So we will hold classes on every fundamental of baseball. Each player will work on nothing but his weakness."[6]

Going into the 1952 season, the third under Matthews, New York Giants manager Leo "The Lip" Durocher sounded off on the Cubs rebuilding program.

"What in the world is Wid Matthews thinking of?" Leo asked. "He keeps saying 'we'll be all right in 1953 if we only can get by this year.'

"But where are those phenoms that are going to turn the Cubs into a winner next year?"[7]

Leo provided a position-by-position rundown of the 1952 Cubs that literally ran down most of the players.

"At first base there's Dee Fondy. Not too bad.

"At second base, Eddie Miksis. Okay. He's a good ballplayer.

"Roy Smalley at short seems to be standing still. He looked like a great prospect once.

"At third there's Ransom Jackson. I like him. He may be a star before he's through.

"In the outfield there's Hank Sauer. Well, Sauer is Sauer.

"Frankie Baumholtz is just an average journeyman."[8]

Leo accused Matthews of sitting tight.

"You can't sit back and wait for a Stan Musial to come along," Leo said. "Just rebuild bit by bit. Before long you've got a ballclub."[9]

Matthews made a ten-player deal with the Pittsburgh Pirates in 1953 for home run king Ralph Kiner and a year and a half later sent him to the Cleveland Indians for pitcher Sam Jones and outfielder Gale Wade. This was perhaps Matthews's best trade as Jones won twenty-three games in his two seasons with the Cubs.

Matthews was credited with bringing in Banks and Gene Baker to break the Cubs' color barrier in September 1953. He also was blamed for not doing it sooner. Baker, the best shortstop in the best league in the minors (the Pacific Coast League) for the Los Angeles Angels, a Cub farm team, waited nearly four years to get a chance.

Going into the 1953 season, Matthews was asked by a Los Angeles sportswriter why Baker was back with the Angels for the fourth straight year.

"It's quite simple," Matthews said. "Baker is a year away from playing major league ball for the Cubs."[10]

The question didn't go away.

"Why are the Cubs delaying a move to bring up Gene Baker, Los Angeles shortstop?" James Enright wrote in the *Chicago American*. "Is it because the 28-year-old Negro isn't ready—or are there other reasons?"[11]

Wendell Smith, a black sportswriter for the *American*, declared, "The most controversial player in the Chicago Cub organization is a 28-year-old shortstop who plays 2,000 miles from here."[12]

Matthews's response to Smith was if the Cubs brought Baker up too soon, it not only hurt his chances in the majors but also the Angels'. This didn't make much sense as both teams were losing and going nowhere in their leagues.

Baker was hitting .282 with twenty homers and ninety-nine RBIs for the Angels when the Cubs finally brought him and Banks up to the majors on September 14, 1953, with eleven games left in the season and

the Cubs in seventh place thirty-seven games behind the league-leading
Dodgers.

"My main thought," Baker later said of his promotion, "was that I
should've been up years before I was."[13]

Baker and Banks were the first blacks I played with in football or
baseball. They could have been polka-dotted. It didn't make any difference to me as long as they went out there and gave all they had and
were nice guys to be around. And they were.

Baker moved to second base and teamed with Banks to become the
first black double-play combination in the major leagues. They were
both named to the 1955 National League All-Star team.

The impact of the dynamic duo on Cub fans like Jerry Pritikin, also
known as the Bleacher Preacher, was immediate.

Jerry was eight years old when he started going to Cub games with
his father in 1945, the last time the Cubs appeared in the World Series.
His father told him about Johnny Kling, a Jewish catcher who played for
the Cubs from 1900 to 1911. Cy Block, a Jewish infielder, had a cup of
coffee with the Cubs in 1945–46.

By 1954 Jerry was seventeen and wondering why the Cubs didn't
have any Jewish players. "If they did, I thought they could sell more
tickets," he said. "The stands were empty very often and sometimes
they closed off the upper deck."

Jerry wrote the Cubs, suggesting they sign a Jewish player to attract
more fans.

"We believe that good ball players will draw people to Wrigley Field
regardless of their color, their race or their religion," Cub business
manager James Gallagher replied in a letter. "We have never exploited
the race or religion of any ball player, nor do we have any intention of
doing so at any time in the future. We could have signed Negro ball
players for the Cubs years ago if we had wanted to do so for the purpose
of exploiting Negroes as gate attractions. We did not do so because we
were not able to find ball players whom we thought could play for the
Cubs, possibly because our scouting system was not as efficient as it
might be, until we did come up with Gene Baker and Ernie Banks."

Gallagher concluded:

"We will follow the same policy as regards Jewish ball players, Cath-
olic ball players, Methodist ball players, Japanese ball players, or any

other ball players. They will be hired and kept solely on the basis of the ability that they show on the playing fields of our great national game."

Gallagher left out Baptist, Presbyterian, and Lutheran players. The Cubs had the same talent pool to draw from as the teams that dominated the National League in the 1950s—the Dodgers, Giants, and Braves. What the Cubs lacked most was leadership with the vision, courage, and judgment needed to build a winning team.

The Cubs had first crack at Jim "Junior" Gilliam, a jack-of-all-trades and master of them all during his fourteen years with the Dodgers in Brooklyn and Los Angeles. In recognition of his playing every position except pitcher and catcher, Junior's glove is enshrined at the National Baseball Hall of Fame in Cooperstown.

Harry Postove, a scout for the Cubs, heralded Gilliam as "the best young prospect in the Negro American League" and recommended his immediate purchase from the Baltimore Elite-Giants.[14]

The teams made a deal after the 1949 season that allowed two Cub farm clubs to look at Gilliam on a trial basis. They concluded Gilliam "wouldn't be able to hit Triple-A pitching."[15]

Gilliam signed with the Dodgers in 1951; batted .301 at Montreal in 1952 to win the Most Valuable Player Award in the Triple-A International League; and in 1953 was the National League Rookie of the Year, enabling Jackie Robinson to move from second to third base, where Jackie primarily played the rest of his career.

Eventually I was traded to the Dodgers, joining Jackie and Junior. Even if it wasn't better for the Cubs than the Sam Jones deal, it was best for me. I went from a team with a habit of losing to one that usually won. I could now go into a game feeling my team was one run up instead of one down. I was no longer wasting away in Wrigleyville.

20

IF YOU CAN'T BEAT 'EM, JOIN 'EM

The Brooklyn Dodgers bullied the Cubs like a ninety-pound weakling, winning sixty-nine of the 109 games during my five full seasons in Chicago. The Cubs never placed higher than fifth, the Dodgers finishing no lower than second. So when the Cubs traded me to the Dodgers on December 6, 1955, it was not only an early Christmas present, it was the best ever.

I was going to the champions of the baseball world, the first and only Brooklyn team to win a World Series. The players were so good that one of them was known only by his first name, Jackie (Robinson), and several others by their nicknames: Pee Wee (Reese), Duke (Snider), Campy (Roy Campanella), Newk (Don Newcombe), Junior (Jim Gilliam), and Oisk (Carl Erskine). They would eventually be celebrated as "The Boys of Summer," endearing themselves to future generations of baseball fans like no other team in history.

If I had asked to be traded, the Dodgers were the team I would've picked. With the Cubs, I hit nineteen of my eighty-seven career home runs against the Dodgers. We still couldn't beat 'em. So I might as well join 'em.

I got the news in a telephone call from a sportswriter friend.

"You've been traded," he said.

"What team?" I asked.

"Take a guess."

Syndicated sports cartoonist Tom Paprocki, who signed his work "Pap," featured Ransom Jackson in this drawing that appeared in newspapers across the United States. Ransom Jackson Collection.

The one team in the National League worse than the Cubs at the time was the Pittsburgh Pirates. Going to Pittsburgh was the equivalent of being shipped to Siberia.

"Pittsburgh."

"Guess again."

The Cincinnati Redlegs usually wound up in the second division so, still expecting the worse, I said, "Cincinnati."

He ended the suspense, saying the Dodgers acquired me in exchange for third baseman Don Hoak and outfielder Walt "Moose" Moryn.

I nearly fainted.

The trade was finalized a few days later, Brooklyn sending pitcher Russ Meyer to the Cubs for Don Elston, another pitcher. The Dodgers not only thought I was worth three players, they were giving me the best chance I'd have to play in a World Series.

Newspaper headlines in big, bold type captured the baseball world's response to the swap.

RIVALS BLAST JACKSON TRADE, one read.[1]

DODGERS GET BEST OF JACKSON DEAL, another concluded.[2]

John P. Carmichael, sports editor of the *Chicago Daily News*, sized up the deal this way: "The Dodgers traded two men, Don Hoak and Walter Moryn whom they didn't need for one man they can use to advantage. In pure paper second-guessing, the world champions packed their already power-laden lineup with a deft, experienced third-baseman and a real, live man at the plate."[3]

I had my differences with Wid Matthews, the Cubs' director of player personnel, but I truly appreciated his sending me to a winning team. He went to the top of my Christmas card list. But my gratitude wasn't widely shared.

"The gag in baseball circles is that Brooklyn Dodger fans are not sending their Christmas letters to Santa, but to Wid Matthews of the Cubs," one columnist cracked.[4]

When Matthews defended the trade by saying the scrappy Hoak would give the Cubs "a little more life and holler," St. Louis Cardinals general manager Frank Lane joked: "I suppose I'll have to get rid of Stan Musial. The guy just isn't the holler type. . . ."[5]

The needling didn't stop there.

If Ransom Jackson had asked to be traded, the Dodgers were the team he would've picked because of a power-packed lineup that featured Duke Snider, Gil Hodges, and Roy Campanella. Left to right are: Snider, Jackson, Hodges, and Campanella. Courtesy Michael Graham.

"Cub fans must look on December 6 as a dark day," one man wrote to a Chicago newspaper. "That's when Wid Matthews bought the Brooklyn Bridge by trading Randy Jackson for Hollerin' Hoak and Waitin' Walt Moryn."[6]

To another fan protesting the trade, Matthews replied: "Please remember that we finished last, seventh and sixth the last three years with Ransom Jackson in the lineup."

The trade prompted Eddie Gold to send friends Christmas cards signed "A former Cub fan."[7]

Eddie worked in the *Chicago Sun-Times* sports department for more than forty-five years and coauthored several books on the Cubs.

"Jackson was THE Cubs," Gold explained at the time. "Without him there is no more Cubs team. He was a pro. I don't know what Hoak and

Moryn are and I may never find out because I won't be in Wrigley Field anymore."[8]

Soon after the trade, I received a welcome letter, dated December 9, from E.J. "Buzzie" Bavasi, vice president and general manager for the Dodgers. "I heard, while I was in Chicago, that you have a tendency to put forth your best efforts only fifty percent of the time," he wrote. "I don't agree with this and was glad to read your statements in the paper yesterday. I know your play next year will justify our making this deal."

I was no more of a fireball than Ernie Banks, my sidekick at short-stop with the Cubs, or my new Dodger teammate, first baseman Gil Hodges. Dodger manager Walter Alston acknowledged this, telling re-porters I walked "kinda slow and unconcerned-like . . . so does Gil Hodges . . . but he gets the job done."[9]

The better job you do, the more games your team wins and the greater the financial rewards for everybody. At least that's what I was thinking as I awaited my first contract offer from the Dodgers.

I made $20,000 a year with the Cubs, who didn't pay diddly-squat. Surely, the world champion Dodgers paid better. I got the contract in the mail and, of course, opened it with bated breath. It was the same amount I got from the Cubs the year before.

I called Buzzie to remind him I had an all-star year with twenty-one homers and seventy runs batted in, despite missing sixteen games. He agreed they were good numbers. "You did all that with the Cubs," he said. "You didn't do anything with the Dodgers."

There was nothing but silence on my end of the line.

"I'll tell you what," he added quickly. "You sound like a nice young man. We'll give you a thousand-dollar raise."

What Buzzie didn't know is that I would've taken fifty cents to go from the Cubs to the Dodgers.

21

JACKIE AND ME

How do you replace a baseball legend and civil rights pioneer—the only man in history to have his number, forty-two, retired by every team in the majors? The answer: you don't.

The Brooklyn Dodgers acquired me from the Chicago Cubs to succeed Jackie Robinson, the greatest all-round baseball player ever.

"Yes, Jackson will play third base," Dodgers vice president Bavasi said in announcing the deal. "It's the only position he plays. And, no, we didn't get him for bench duty."[1]

I was thirty years old at the time—seven years younger than Jackie.

I was in college in 1947 when Jackie became the first African American to play in the big leagues.

I was in the minors in 1949 when he won the National League Most Valuable Player Award, leading the league with a .342 batting average and thirty-seven stolen bases.

I was so absorbed in my own career that when I reached the majors in 1950, I had yet to appreciate Jackie's greatness. He was just another player I had to compete against.

There are a few guys that come along that have everything. Jackie was one of them. He was the ultimate ballplayer, one that transcends all of the statistics used to measure performance. On all-time lists, his career batting average of .311 barely ranks in the top hundred while nearly 350 players have topped his 197 stolen bases. The most home runs he hit in a single season was nineteen.

What Jackie did better than anybody else was beat you. And he could do it with a glove or bat as well as his throwing arm, legs, and head. "This guy didn't just come to play," New York Giants manager Leo Durocher once said of Jackie. "He came to beat ya. He come to stuff the goddamn bat right up your ass."[2]

Playing third base meant I was dangerously close to Jackie's bat. I had to be close enough to discourage him from bunting for an easy hit but if I got too close, one of his vicious line drives was likely to reshape my head. I was ready for anything.

He ran the bases like the track and football star he was at UCLA, once stealing his way around the bases—second, third, and home. He stole home twenty times in his career, including the 1955 World Series. The last person I wanted to see dancing around second base was Jackie. I knew he was coming.

On one occasion, Jackie was on second and Pee Wee Reese on third. When a pitched ball got away from the catcher, Pee Wee took off for home. On realizing he wasn't going to make it, Pee Wee headed back to third where I had taken the throw from the catcher and was waiting with the ball. Straddling the bag, I tagged out a sliding Pee Wee first and, then, flipped my glove over to nab Jackie, sliding in from second.

He played every position in the infield for the Dodgers except short-stop, and he was an all-star there for the Kansas City Monarchs in the Negro Leagues.

I didn't like playing against Jackie. It wasn't a black-white thing. I had to have the same mind-set he did or else I was going to get a bat in an unwanted place. I might love him afterward but not during the game.

Now, Jackie was a teammate and, as I eventually found out, a nice guy. But we were still battling each other, this time for the same job.

I was coming off of back-to-back All-Star Game appearances with the Cubs and determined to prove I belonged on a star-packed Dodger team that won the 1955 World Series.

Jackie was out to show the Dodgers and media skeptics that he was not over the hill. Injuries forced him to miss nearly a third of the team's games in 1955. His batting average dropped fifty-five points from the year before to a career-low .256. I didn't know it at the time, but the Dodgers slashed Jackie's salary by $5,000—from $40,000 to $35,000.

Jackie was overweight, and his body was showing the wear and tear of all the punishment it took and dished out on the field. He was fighting for his job and on the ropes. The media smelled blood and treated my competition with Jackie like it was a prize fight against another famous Robinson, Sugar Ray, the reigning world middleweight champion.

It was Robby vs. Jackson, Ransom vs. Jackie, or Jack vs. Jackson, pick your favorite headline.

"I regard myself as fortunate to having a third base fight between Jackson and Robinson scheduled for the training season," Dodger manager Walter Alston said at the start of spring training in Vero Beach, Florida.[3]

When I arrived a few days later, I was asked to respond to a comment by Jackie that he was a better third baseman than me when he was in good shape.

"I don't mind a good fight," I said. "Over the years, Jackie has been a great player."

There was no fight or feud, but it was entertaining reading.

"Ransom Jackson will have to be a whale of a player this year to beat me out," Jackie told a wire-service reporter. "It'll mean that we have that much stronger a team, and make us a cinch to win the pennant. I'll wish him good luck and be his substitute. But Jackson will have to beat me at my best."[4]

Jackie reported to Vero Beach weighing 212 pounds, the lowest in years, and in excellent condition. "My legs are strong, and that's the main thing," he said.[5]

I played half the spring exhibition games, Jackie the other half. Alston let us battle it out while keeping everyone guessing.

"No matter who plays third, Jackson or Robinson, I know we'll have a helluva man playing third base for us this season," he said. "A good problem is no problem."[6]

Jackie didn't wait for Alston to announce his decision.

"The skipper hasn't said anything either way," Jackie said two weeks before the season opened. "But the way I feel, I've won the job. I'm not taking anything away from Randy. I've got a lot of respect for his ability, but I've got more respect for my own."[7]

Shortly before our first game, Alston called me into his office at Ebbets Field. "Jackie has been here a long time and deserves to start," he said.

"I haven't been disappointed in Jackson at all," Alston explained to reporters. "He has played well. But Robinson has been terrific. When he sets his mind to it, he can beat anyone out of a job."[8]

I expected Jackie to start all along and completely agreed with Alston's decision. It was the right thing to do.

Looking back, my situation was similar to an actor, a star in some circles, getting a chance to be in a movie with far bigger stars like John Wayne, William Holden, Burt Lancaster, Gary Cooper, and Marilyn Monroe. I had a conversation with the director that went like this:

"You're going to be the sheriff who shows up once during the movie and you get shot at the end."

"Great, man, that's fine with me."

The Brooklyn Dodgers acquired Ransom Jackson, left, to replace thirty-seven-year-old Jackie Robinson at third base, but a fired-up and slimmed-down Jackie was the starter to begin the 1956 season. Ransom Jackson Collection.

The way I figured it, people would be talking about who shot the sheriff and, perhaps, even the sheriff.

Jackie had done everything for the Dodgers; I had done nothing.

With the Cubs, I was one of a sprinkling of stars with a small "s." The Dodgers had a dozen Stars with a big "S." I didn't know when my time would come, but I didn't mind sitting on the bench and watching an all-star cast until it did.

I started only one game in April and had nineteen at bats going into a game against the Pittsburgh Pirates May 29. Meanwhile, Jackie was struggling with a .250 batting average. Alston came to me and said, "It's your turn."

I got three hits against the Pirates, and two days later I had another three-hit game against my old team, the Cubs, at Wrigley Field. Batting fourth in the cleanup position between Duke Snider and Gil Hodges, I went on a rampage the first half of June. During one stretch, I went nineteen-for-forty-nine to raise my batting average to .351. I was driving in a run per game.

"I'd like to get back in but the way Jackson is going, he certainly deserves to stay there," Jackie said. [9]

The highlight of the month and the season was a game against the Philadelphia Phillies June 29 at Ebbets Field. "Just say that it will go down in the annals of Dodger history," a press box attendee said to a sportswriter looking for the right words to describe what happened in the bottom of the ninth inning. [10] Dick Young of the *New York Daily News* didn't need any help. He wrote:

> Pretty soon nobody's going to watch the Ebbets Field show any more, not even on TV. They keep running the same tired old movie over and over again—only the ending gets more and more preposterous. Last night, it winds up with the bad guys from Philly having the good guys from Brooklyn hopelessly surrounded at Fort Ebbets, and there's only two outs left. Then, bing, bing, bing, just like that, three straight homers by Snider, Jackson and Hodges, and the good guys win the whole thing, 6–5. Ain't that asking you to believe a lot? [11]

It was the third time in eight days we scored three or more runs in the bottom of the ninth to turn certain defeat into victory.

Only once before in nearly a hundred thousand major-league games had any team belted three successive homers in the ninth. Never had it been done by the last three batters in a game.

"Three home runs in a row on four pitches," Duke Snider said. "Wow!"

"Then I'm sorry I took that curve for ball," I said in jest. [12]

The Phillies were leading 5–2 entering the ninth. Jim Gilliam walked. Pee Wee Reese struck out.

Up to the plate walked Duke. Bing! The ball sailed over a screen in right field.

The Phillies changed pitchers, replacing junk-baller Stu Miller with hard-throwing Jack Meyer.

I watched the first pitch go by for a ball. On the next pitch I let it rip—bing! The ball shot into the left-center-field seats. The score was now tied 5–5 with Gil Hodges coming to bat.

Gil swung at the first pitch. Bing!

"What a finish," I said after the game. "Who's that guy from Yale? Frank Merriwell, that's it." [13]

Merriwell was a fictional sports hero in the early 1900s made popular by books, radio dramas, and a film series. I was feeling a little like Merriwell myself.

Going into the three-day break for Major League Baseball's All-Star Game July 10, the Dodgers were in third place with a 42–32 won-loss record, only two games behind league-leading Cincinnati. I was hitting .294, helping win games in dramatic Merriwell fashion.

The Dodgers' super-statistician Allan Roth had devised a way to measure how a hitter performs with runners on second and third base. My scoring position average was a lofty .359.

Taking a shower at home one night, I suffered a bad gash on my left thumb when the porcelain faucet knob snapped off in my hand as I was turning off the water. The wound required three large stitches and caused me to miss the next thirteen games.

Long after the thumb healed, I had trouble gripping a bat. I was unable to recapture the Merriwell magic, and my batting average slipped to a season-ending .272. The irony in all this is that I could handle the best fastball pitchers of the time but not a water faucet knob.

Jackie returned to third base and finished the season strong, hitting .275 with ten home runs.

Walter Alston, rear, was a happy manager after Duke Snider, far left, Ransom Jackson, far right, and Gil Hodges, center, hit three straight homers in the ninth inning to give the Brooklyn Dodgers a come-from-behind 6–5 victory. It was the first time in big-league history that the last three batters in a game homered. Ransom Jackson Collection.

When I started at third, Jackie often played second or first. One of my most vivid memories of the 1956 season is Jackie clapping his hands as I slid into home plate to complete a rare inside-the-park home run at Ebbets Field. The scene symbolized our support of each other.

We were competitors, not rivals. We knew the situation and never talked about it. Instead, we discussed opposing players—how to defend the hitters and hit the pitchers.

I'll never know what Jackie experienced breaking baseball's color barrier because he never mentioned it.

We were both college graduates and had to deal with a stereotype prevalent at the time that college-educated players considered themselves superior to everybody else. The subject never came up.

Jackie Robinson, number forty-two, claps his hands as Ransom Jackson completes a rare inside-the-park home run at Brooklyn's Ebbets Field. Jackie scored on Ransom's three-run blast to deep center. Ransom Jackson Collection.

There was plenty of speculation that Jackie would retire after the 1956 season, but he never said anything about it.

Players in the 1950s generally didn't know the salaries of other players, so I wasn't aware the Dodgers tried to cut Jackie's salary $7,000 until recently. Jackie agreed to $5,000. I got mad when I found out; Jackie never complained.

I was watching from the bench on the last day of the season when Jackie homered to help beat the Pittsburgh Pirates and clinch the National League pennant. The champagne flowed as we toasted each other on a Merriwell ending that saw us win three straight while the Milwaukee Braves lost two of their final three games. That was the difference—one game.

Jackie started all seven games in the 1956 World Series and played regularly in the Dodgers' month-long tour of Japan that followed. He didn't announce his retirement until after he was traded to the Dodgers' archrivals, the New York Giants.

Six years later, in 1962, Jackie was inducted into the National Base-ball Hall of Fame. In 2013, the movie *42* brought back to life the competitive fire and courage he showed on and off the diamond. It was a thrill to play against Jackie; it was a greater thrill playing with him.

22

A MASTERPIECE (AND A FLUKE)

The most popular television show in 1956 was *The Ed Sullivan Show*.

On Sunday, September 9, 1956, a record sixty million viewers—nearly 83 percent of the TV audience that night—watched Elvis Presley shake, rattle, and roll.

Three weeks later I was on the show along with my Brooklyn Dodger teammates and the New York Yankee players we would face in the World Series starting the following Wednesday. It was old hat for many of them as this was the sixth series in ten years for the two teams. But it was a first for me.

As I was standing backstage at Ed Sullivan Theater in New York City waiting to walk out and be introduced by Sullivan, all I could think of was, "This wouldn't be happening if I was still with the Cubs."

It seemed unreal because when I woke up Sunday morning, the Dodgers and Milwaukee Braves were tied for first place in the National League. If we both won, there would be a playoff. A loss meant I cleaned out my locker and headed home like past seasons with the Cubs.

We beat the Pittsburgh Pirates at Ebbets Field. Now, we had to wait for the Braves to finish their game in St. Louis against the Cardinals. We hung around the dugout and clubhouse, still in our uniforms, listening to a radio broadcast of the game.

The Braves lost. We won the pennant and were going to the World Series. I had to get a newspaper Monday morning to see if it was really true.

Immediately after the Brooklyn Dodgers won their last game of the 1956 season to clinch a tie for the National League pennant, pitcher Carl Erskine, left, and owner Walter O'Malley, right, crowded around Ransom Jackson to listen to the Milwaukee Braves–St. Louis Cardinals game on the radio. The Cards won, making the Dodgers champs. Ransom Jackson Collection.

I wasn't sure Sunday night at the Ed Sullivan Theater.

Lucy and Desi Arnaz did a comedy routine. Elvis wasn't around, so Gisele MacKenzie sang "Canadian Sunset" and a Swedish boys choir performed a marching song.

Now it was time for Sullivan to interview the Yankees' Yogi Berra and the Dodgers' Sal Maglie and for the rest of us to march across the stage and shake hands with Ed.

My personal goals in the majors were the same as most players. One was to play in an All-Star Game. Another was to win the pennant, and the third was to participate in a World Series. I never imagined being on *The Ed Sullivan Show*, the longest-running TV variety show in history (twenty-three years) and the launchpad in 1963 for the Beatles and Beatlemania in the United States.

The dream continued into the World Series.

Just before the start of the first game at Ebbets Field, President Dwight D. Eisenhower stood near the Dodger dugout, shaking hands and wishing the players good luck as they filed past.

The 1956 presidential elections were the next month. Running against President Eisenhower was former governor Adlai Stevenson of Illinois, the Democratic Party candidate.

Governor Stevenson attended the second game, sitting in the front row behind the Dodger dugout. The governor and my father were classmates at Princeton University in the 1920s. I was in the locker room when a clubhouse attendant announced, "The governor wants to meet you, Randy."

I hurried out to give Governor Stevenson a baseball signed by the entire Dodger team. Hopefully, he took better care of it than the autographed baseball I received as a kid from Hall of Famer Bill Dickey.

The 1956 World Series is best remembered for the perfect game pitched by the Yankees' Don Larsen—the only one in World Series history. Twenty-seven guys up; twenty-seven down. It was a masterpiece, like the *Mona Lisa* and the Seventh Symphony. It also was a fluke.

That's the only word to describe a feat so rare that it's estimated the odds of pitching a perfect game in the majors today are one in nearly thirty thousand. Multiply that several times and you've got the chances of anybody repeating what Larsen did on baseball's biggest stage.

I've had sixty years to think about Larsen's amazing achievement. When I do, I'm reminded of "Bobo's No-No," the name given the no-hitter by the Cub reject, Lee "Bobo" Holloman of the St. Louis Browns in 1953.

Bobo's No-No was far from perfect. He walked five batters and muffed a grounder for an error. Browns owner Bill Veeck described it as "the quaintest no-hitter in the history of the game" as would-be homers "curved foul at the last second" and "a bunt just rolled foul on the last spin."[1]

"Big Bobo Holloman was one with the immortals," Veeck said. "Even among immortals, Big Bobo was immortal; he was the only pitcher in the twentieth century to pitch a no-hit game on his first major-league start."[2]

In 1892 a pitcher tossed a no-hitter in his first big-league start, but Bobo is the only other guy to do it. He won two more times in the majors and didn't complete another game.

Bobo and Larsen were teammates with the Browns in 1953. On the same pitching staff were veterans Leroy "Satchel" Paige, Virgil "Fire" Trucks, Harry "The Cat" Brecheen, and "Bullet Bob" Turley.

Paige claimed he threw fifty no-hitters in the Negro Leagues, and who's to dispute it? Trucks hurled two no-hitters the year before for the Detroit Tigers. Brecheen was a twenty-game winner for the Cardinals in 1948, and Turley was a future Cy Young Award winner for the Yankees.

Nobody would've picked Bobo from this group to pitch a no-hitter any more than Larsen would've been singled out as the Yankee to pitch the only perfect game in World Series history dating back to 1903. The perfecto by Larsen was every bit as improbable as Bobo's No-No.

Of all the Yankee and Dodger starting pitchers, Larsen was the least likely to join Bobo in the Hall of the Immortals.

The Yankee ace in 1956 was Charles "Whitey" Ford, a nineteen-game winner with an outstanding 2.47 earned run average. Johnny Kucks won eighteen games and Tom Sturdivant sixteen.

The Dodgers had Don Newcombe (27–7), Sal Maglie (13–5), Carl Erskine (13–11), and Roger Craig (12–11). Erskine had two no-hitters in his career, and Maglie tossed a no-hitter in the last week of the 1956 season. In the Dodger bullpen were two future Hall of Famers: nineteen-year-old Don Drysdale and twenty-year-old Sandy Koufax, who pitched four no-hitters, including a perfect game, in his brilliant career. Only Nolan Ryan with seven has more.

Larsen won eleven games for the Yankees during the regular season, but two years earlier he had a 3–21 won-loss record for the Baltimore Orioles.

The Dodgers treated him like he was still with the Orioles. In the fourth game of the 1955 World Series, he was roughed up for five runs in four innings, two of them homers. It was more of the same in 1956, Larsen unable to make it past the second inning of the second game, blowing a six-run lead.

The best-of-seven series was tied after four games. Pitching against Larsen in game five was Maglie, the cagey veteran who beat the Yankees in the series opener. We liked our chances. They were far better than the odds of a perfect game by Larsen.

Bobo's No-No was against the Philadelphia Athletics, described by Veeck as "the softest competition we could find."[3]

Larsen was facing a Dodger lineup featuring four players now in the Hall of Fame—Jackie Robinson, Pee Wee Reese, Duke Snider, and Roy Campanella.

As they walked to the plate, Bob Sheppard, the public-address announcer at Yankee Stadium, called out their names in a reverential tone that earned him the nickname "The Voice of God."

"Now batting for the Dodgers, the third baseman, number forty-two, Jackie Robinson, number forty-two."

I was on the bench watching helplessly as Larsen cruised along—one-two-three for six straight innings. In the seventh, we finally realized what was happening, and we couldn't believe it. We weren't alone.

"If Nolan Ryan had done it, if Sandy Koufax had done it, if Don Drysdale had done it, I would have nodded and said, 'Well, it could happen,'" Sheppard said in 2002 on ESPN Classic's *SportsCentury* series. "But Don Larsen?"[4]

I played in two no-hit games for the Cubs, the one Sam "Toothpick" Jones pitched for us and the other Erskine threw against us. When a no-hitter is being pitched against you, it's a shock. Each out adds more tension and stress.

With two outs in the ninth inning, the only thing between the right-handed Larsen and baseball immortality was the pinch hitter Dodger manager Walt Alston picked to bat against him. It would either be me, a right-hander, or Dale Mitchell, a left-hander.

I didn't like to pinch-hit, probably because I wasn't one of those guys who could fall out of bed in the middle of the night, grab a bat, and rip line drives. My first home run in the majors was as a pinch hitter and I belted another one with the Cleveland Indians near the end of my career, but they were the exception.

Up to that point in the series, I was hitless in three pinch-hit attempts. Mitchell was 0-for-2.

I fouled out in the second game, flied out in the third, and was called out on strikes in the fourth. I'm still upset about that one.

The bases were loaded with one out in the ninth inning, the Dodgers trailing 6–2. A grand-slam homer tied the game.

Ransom Jackson was visibly upset after being called out on strikes in the ninth inning of the 1956 World Series. Jackson thought the pitch was high and should've been ball four. Several television viewers wrote to tell Jackson he was right, it was a bad call. Ransom Jackson Collection.

There were a few times in my career I went up to the plate trying to hit a home run out of necessity. I succeeded once against the Cubs' Jim Brosnan. He kept throwing high fastballs and I fouled them off until finally I belted one out of the park.

I wasn't thinking home run this time. My job was to get on base and keep the rally going. The count was full—three balls and two strikes. The next pitch was just above the letters on my uniform, one that I had taken a thousand times for a ball. Larry Napp, an American League umpire, didn't agree. "Strike three!" he hollered.

In the 1950s, umpires in the National League had a lower strike zone, calling pitches just above the knee a strike and anything above the letters a ball. Those same pitches were called differently by American League umps. A lot of fans who watched the game on television wrote to tell me that it was a bad call.

Mitchell had a lifetime batting average of .312 and was a great contact hitter. In 4,358 plate appearances, he struck out a mere 119 times. He batted against Larsen in the second game and fouled out.

I wanted to hear "The Voice of God" call my name. You play the game for moments like this. Whatever happened would be historic. Instead, Alston played the percentages and sent Mitchell to the plate.

"Now pinch-hitting for the Dodgers," Sheppard announced, "number eight, Dale Mitchell, number eight."

Mitchell worked the count to one ball and two strikes. He fouled off the next pitch. And then he watched a fastball zoom past. Umpire Babe Pinelli called it strike three. Dale thought it was high and outside and whirled around to protest. In a bit of irony befitting Larsen's masterpiece, the game ended with perhaps the toughest hitter in baseball to strike out looking at a called third strike.

"They can never break my record," Larsen said afterward. "The best they can do is tie it."[5]

It will take another masterpiece (and a fluke), and Larsen knows that the chances of that happening are virtually zero.

When Mitchell died in 1987, the lead paragraph of his obituary in the *New York Times* mentioned he made the final out in Larsen's perfect game. They will be linked forever, even in death.

We bounced back to win the sixth game and then lost the deciding seventh game. The defining moment of the series, however, was Larsen's "well-timed masterpiece."[6]

President Dwight D. Eisenhower is shown chatting with Ransom Jackson in this shot taken before the first game of the 1956 World Series. President Eisenhower signed the photo for Jackson. Ransom Jackson Collection.

That's what the *New York Times* called it, reporting: "The unpredictable Larsen had triumphed at a time when the Bombers needed it most. . . ."[7]

The everlasting image is Don cradling Yogi in his arms after the final out.

Fortunately, I have another picture to remind me of the 1956 World Series.

A couple of months later I received a photograph of me shaking President Eisenhower's hand. In turn, I sent it to the White House, asking him to autograph it. The signed photo and accompanying letter are framed and displayed prominently on a wall near my favorite chair at home. I only wish there was a shot of me with Ed Sullivan. Those are better memories for an old Dodger.

23

KINGS IN JAPAN

The New York Yankees beat the Brooklyn Dodgers in the 1956 World Series, but it was the Dodgers who were treated like kings in a month-long tour of Japan.

Everywhere we went there were "Welcome B Dodgers" signs and parades with confetti and balloons flying around us in the backseats of the convertibles we rode in. On arriving in Tokyo, some hundred thousand onlookers lined the streets in a light, drizzling rain to cheer our twenty-six-car motorcade as it traveled from Haneda Airport to the Imperial Hotel downtown.

From Tokyo we went to Sapporo, Sendai, Mito, Kofu, Utsunomiya, Fukuoka, Shimonoseki, Hiroshima, Osaka, Gifu, Nagoya, and Shizuoka before returning to Tokyo and Fukuoka. Altogether, we visited thirteen cities. Except for Tokyo and Hiroshima, they were places most of us had never heard of, let alone could pronounce.

We played nineteen games in front of more than 450,000 fans, an average of around twenty-four thousand per game. That topped the 15,761 the Dodgers averaged at home in 1956 and slightly below Milwaukee's major-league high of 26,576.

The Dodgers' goodwill tour was the third by a big-league team since World War II ended in 1945. The New York Giants visited in 1953 followed by the Yankees in 1955.

The day after losing the seventh game of the World Series to the Yankees, we boarded a chartered Pan American DC7 aircraft at New York City's Idlewild Airport to fly to Honolulu, Hawaii, for three exhibition games and then on to Tokyo with an eight-hour stopover on Wake Island to fix a couple of flat tires. "If there is anything we can do to make your flight more pleasant, let us know," a flight attendant announced as we started the journey. "By the way, my name is Miss Larsen."[1]

We wanted to forget the perfect game the Yankees' Don Larsen pitched against us, and the Japanese fans helped us do that. They loved baseball, and they knew all about the Brooklyn Dodgers and Jackie Robinson, Duke Snider, and Sal Maglie, some of our big stars. They were disappointed that Maglie stayed home, but not for long as a kid pitcher named Don Drysdale wowed them with his physical size and devastating fastball.

At six foot six, Don already was "Big D" on the mound. He threw sidearm, kind of herky-jerky, and the ball sank toward right-handed batters, sometimes breaking their bats. He was intimidating and beginning to show the dominance that enabled him to win 209 games in the majors.

Don's won-loss record was 5–5 in 1956, his first year in the big leagues. A twenty-year-old left-hander, Sandy Koufax, was 2–4. They were both wild. When they pitched batting practice, I skipped it and found something else to do. I could tell they had a great future because they made me doubt my own. Hall of Famer Orlando Cepeda best described Don: "The trick against Drysdale is to hit him before he hits you."[2]

We lost two of the first three games, the most losses by any big-league club on a Japanese tour. The Yankees were 15–0–1 and the Giants 14–1–1. We finished with a 14–4–1 record. "It would not be an overstatement to say that we no longer have anything to learn from the Dodgers," the former manager of one Japanese team said.[3]

"The Dodgers looked on the trip as a holiday," explained Vin Scully, longtime radio voice of the Dodgers. "But the Japanese looked on it as a crusade, and they played to win."[4]

The Japanese teams had something to prove. They were made up primarily of all-stars from the country's two professional leagues. I was impressed with their speed and how much ground they covered on defense. The one big weakness was a dearth of power hitters, but they made up for that by spraying hits all over the field.

In Osaka, veteran American umpire Jocko Conlan tried stopping the game after six innings because of darkness and a light drizzle. Nearly forty thousand fans protested with chants of "Yaro!"—Play ball! The game continued with the Dodgers scoring seven runs in the eighth to win 14–7.

In Tokyo, a pitcher for the Yomiuri Giants ignored his manager's decision to intentionally walk Jackie with a runner on second, and the game tied 4–4 in the eleventh inning. Jackie doubled in the winning run.

In Shimonoseki, Gino Cimoli hit a line-drive shot up the middle that careened off the pitcher's head into the right-field corner for a triple. We were shocked that the pitcher wasn't knocked down and out by the blow. He was removed from the game but, as all Japanese pitchers did, he threw about fifteen pitches in front of the dugout before continuing to the locker room.

We spent two nights on trains sleeping in beds so small that Drysdale had to lie on his side with his legs pulled up high in a fetal position. It was a sight that would've endeared him even more to his new fan club of young Japanese girls.

In Sapporo the hotel where we stayed didn't have enough rooms so some of the players slept on the floor.

On one flight the plane was about to touch down when, suddenly, it shot up and to the left before circling and landing safely. When we got off the plane, one of the American servicemen at the airport told us we were lucky because the plane was about to crash into the terminal before it veered away.

Emotions were high as we arrived in Hiroshima late one afternoon for a game the next day.

On August 6, 1945, Hiroshima was reduced to a virtual wasteland by the world's first atom bomb dropped from an American B-29 bomber, the *Enola Gay*. The blast killed 140,000 people. Approximately two-thirds of Hiroshima's ninety thousand buildings were destroyed.

Eleven years had passed and thousands of the buildings had been replaced. The ballpark was new. But there was no replacing the people who lost their lives. For those who survived, there was no forgetting.

The players were told not to go out alone at night. If we left the hotel, it should be in pairs or threesomes. Drysdale and I roomed to-

A memorable and poignant moment of the Brooklyn Dodgers' goodwill tour of Japan in 1956 was a visit to a memorial in Hiroshima honoring the victims of the atomic bomb dropped on the city near the end of World War II. Front row, left to right, are Sotaro Suzuki, the *Yomiuri Shimbun* sportswriter who helped coordinate the tour; Fresco Thompson, a Dodger vice president; Pee Wee Reese, team captain; Walter Alston, manager; and Dick Walsh, secretary of the Dodgers' minor-league operations. Visible in the background are Don Drysdale, far left; Jackie Robinson; Don Zimmer; Clem Labine (behind Reese); Bob Aspromonte (next to Labine); and Gino Cimoli (behind Alston on far right). Ransom Jackson Collection.

gether in Japan. We stayed in the lobby of the hotel where we talked with a receptionist and bellman who were in their early twenties.

"Where were you when the bomb was dropped?" I asked.

They said a couple of weeks before the bombing, American planes dropped leaflets in the area telling residents to go to the nearby mountains for safety because something terrible was going to happen.

"Our families took it very seriously," one of them said. "We went up in the mountains along with a lot of other people. We lived through the blast and that's why we're here today."

I mentioned the story in a speech in Georgia many years later and a man told me afterwards with tears in his eyes, "I was a gunner on one of the planes that dropped the leaflets. Keep telling that story."

Recently, the news media has challenged the leaflets story, claiming they were dropped *after* Hiroshima was bombed. The young people who credited the warning leaflets with saving their lives—and the man in Georgia—had no reason to make up the story, so I'll always believe them.

The morning of the game in Hiroshima, Dodger executives and players visited a memorial to the bombing victims and dedicated a bronze plaque near the entrance to Hiroshima Stadium. Inscribed on the plaque are these words: "We dedicate this visit in memory of those baseball fans and others who here died by atomic action on August 6, 1945. May their souls rest in peace and with God's help and man's resolution peace will prevail forever, amen."[5]

The Japanese people gave us the royal treatment, but they were the real kings in Japan. They rebuilt their cities, transformed their country, and created a lasting peace. Today, Japanese baseball is respected worldwide and consistently produces major-league stars. And Japanese baseball fans are as passionate today as they were in 1956.

24

BUMMER OF A SEASON

Jackie Robinson was gone; third base was mine. All I had to do was stay healthy.

After three straight seasons of freakish hand injuries, I figured the worst was over and playing every day I could hit around .300 and twenty-something home runs.

Injuries are as much a part of baseball as any of the mind-numbing statistics used to measure a player's performance. They can make or break careers.

A broken wrist to Bill Serena in 1951 was a turning point for both of us as it sidelined Bill for the rest of the season and suddenly made me the Chicago Cubs' starting third baseman. Bill played three more years for the Cubs, mostly as a backup at third and second base. His career ended in the minors in 1957.

I was hitting .310 with sixteen homers entering the 1954 All-Star Game in Cleveland.

Earlier in the year Ty Cobb, "The Georgia Peach" and one of the greatest players of all time, told Phil Cavarretta, then Cub manager, "You know who I like on your ball club? Randy Jackson. The kid is going to be a real good hitter within another year or two."[1]

I was on the road to stardom, or so it appeared.

As I went to field a hard-hit grounder in the All-Star Game, the ball took a bad bounce and instinctively I put my bare right hand in front of my face for protection. The middle finger became infected and my hand so swollen that I could hardly throw the ball or grip the bat. Over

This photo of Ransom Jackson with Hall of Famer Ty Cobb at his home in Royston, Georgia, was taken long after Cobb predicted stardom for Jackson, who was plagued by injuries throughout his career. Left to right are Dr. Wayne Satterfield of Athens, Georgia; Frank Sinkwich, 1942 Heisman Trophy winner from the University of Georgia; Cobb; and Jackson. Ransom Jackson Collection.

the next eighteen games, my batting average dropped seventeen points to .293.

We were in Pittsburgh when the Pirates' team doctor examined the hand and decided a little surgery was in order. As I held my hand flat on a table in the training room, he took a scalpel and made a one-inch gash in the hand and squeezed it. It was the closest I ever came to fainting.

Whatever the doctor was looking for, he didn't find it. The Cubs immediately sent me to Chicago where I was hospitalized and treated for blood poisoning. I missed three weeks and struggled at the plate the rest of the season, winding up with a .273 average.

I was hitting at a torrid .450 pace through the first five games of 1955 when an infection to the same hand put me back in the hospital. This time the diagnosis was a spider bite. It happened either in a hotel room or the Cub clubhouse at Sportsman's Park where we were playing the Cardinals at the time. I was out two weeks and never got back into my season-opening groove, despite a career-high twenty-one homers.

The weirdest of this unholy trinity of injuries was the thumb I gashed while turning off the porcelain faucet knob in the shower at home during the All-Star Game break. I went from batting cleanup for the Dodgers to sitting on the bench. One sportswriter suggested I should stay out of bathrooms instead of barrooms.

Accidents happen in threes, right?

The Dodgers were the first major-league team to switch from trains to planes, rolling out in 1957 a forty-four-passenger Convair 440 Metropolitan.

Nobody gave much thought to three incidents that happened during spring training. Looking back, they are more ominous, a sign perhaps of the season ahead.

After playing our final exhibition game in Florida, we were scheduled to travel from Jacksonville to the Texas cities of San Antonio, Houston, Dallas, and Fort Worth, and then north to Oklahoma City and Tulsa; Wichita, Kansas; and Kansas City, Missouri.

As we prepared to depart Jacksonville, it was announced that the weight of forty-four passengers and equipment was too much for the new plane and we'd have to carry less gas and land in New Orleans, Louisiana, for refueling instead of flying nonstop to San Antonio.

"It's a minor problem, however," the chief pilot said, "and during the season, when the club doesn't carry all those bats and balls, we can go with a full load of gas."[2]

A week later mechanical trouble caused a two-hour delay in our flight from Oklahoma City to Tulsa. We arrived twenty-five minutes before game time, followed ten minutes later by our uniforms that apparently were bused to Tulsa with the equipment.

The next day in Wichita I hit a home run, my second of the spring, and in Kansas City I belted a double and a triple. Earlier in the month, I had six extra-base hits in five exhibition games to clinch Jackie's old job.

After the game in Kansas City against the Athletics, we would fly back to Brooklyn. First, we had to survive playing the A's in weather conditions better suited for the Abominable Snowman. It was thirty-eight degrees Fahrenheit when the afternoon game started and thirty-three at the end, snow flurries swirling around the field.

"After all, what can you expect when you play Brooklyn?" a shivering Kansas City fan said. "I wouldn't be surprised if they put in a penguin to play third base."[3]

I might've taken that personally but I was too busy trying to avoid frostbite.

"Man, it's so cold you have to look twice to see if you've got the ball," Dodger second baseman Jim Gilliam said of catching the ball with cold-deadened hands.[4]

"When I hit that ball, it felt like I had a handful of bumblebees," explained A's outfielder Gus Zernial.[5]

Vic Power of the A's was running from first to second when a ball thrown by Dodger shortstop Don Zimmer hit him in the head, knocking him unconscious and causing a concussion.

Late in the game I could hear sounds from the A's bullpen that quickly got my attention. Wham! Wham! Wham! The ball was banging wildly against a metal backstop.

I looked out there and saw Ryne Duren warming up. Duren wore dark, Coke-bottle-thick glasses, and he had a blazing fastball that he was never sure where it was going.

"If he could see better," wrote Jim Murray, *Los Angeles Times* sports columnist, "he'd be just another guy with a fastball. This way, he's a one-man war-of-nerves."[6]

I could barely distinguish the ball from the snowflakes whipping around as I got ready to face Duren, leading off the top of the ninth inning. We were ahead 4–1. Most of the crowd of 8,531 had already gone home. I didn't want to leave the field on a stretcher like Power.

I walked up to Ed Runge, the home plate umpire.

"Would you call every pitch a strike and let's get out of here?"

"I'd be glad to," Ed said.

The first pitch whisked past my chin.

"Strike one!"

The next one wasn't even close to the plate.

"Strike two!"

The third pitch was high again.

"Strike three!" Ed bellowed. "You're out of here."

Ed did the same thing for the next two batters. Duren struck out the side, and the A's scored four runs in the bottom of the ninth to win, 5–4.

We were more concerned with getting out of Kansas City and back to Brooklyn for the regular-season opener.

The only problem was the team's new Convair couldn't go anywhere until its wings were de-iced. We landed at New York City's LaGuardia Airport at three o'clock in the morning after what the *New York Herald-Tribune* called "eight and a half hours of imprisonment (more than half of this on the snow-covered ground of the Kansas City airport) in their costly Convair. . . ."[7]

We didn't have any more plane troubles, but we had plenty on the playing field.

Eight games into the season at Pittsburgh I hit a ground ball to third and was running to first base like I had done thousands of times. The throw to Pirate first baseman Frank Thomas was high and wide, forcing Frank to make a leaping catch and come down on top of me as my left foot was about to hit the bag.

I was examined in the locker room by the same guy who played doctor with my infected hand three years before. I'd intentionally forgotten his name but not the bloody mess he made of my hand. I couldn't get on the plane to Brooklyn for X-rays and treatment fast enough.

The impact from the collision bent back my left knee, tearing the cartilage. I didn't play again until mid-July, starting only twenty-four more games and finishing with a .197 batting average, two home runs, and sixteen runs batted in.

Pee Wee Reese and Zimmer took over at third base while Charlie Neal filled in for Pee Wee at shortstop.

The injury was one of many that had the Dodger locker room looking like a hospital ward. Pee Wee was nagged by back and leg problems; Duke Snider played with a brace on his left knee; and pitchers Carl Erskine, Sal Maglie, Sandy Koufax, and Clem Labine all missed action because of sore throwing arms.

A story in the July 31, 1957, issue of *Sporting News* listed thirty-one injuries, including this rundown for one day, May 30: "Reese pulled a leg muscle and suffered what was called 'an evulsion fracture in the rib region.' Rube Walker cut his right hand and had to have stitches. Sal Maglie, fielding fungoes, suffered a slight fracture and dislocation of his right thumb. Carl Furillo had a stiff neck, a stomach disturbance and right arm trouble. Later, when the stiff neck healed, Carl pulled a ligament in his left shoulder."[8]

Through sixty games, Dodger manager Walt Alston used fifty-five different starting lineups.

Late-inning rallies that produced magical victories the year before now fizzled. Alston pushed all the buttons trying to put more runs on the scoreboard.

In the ninth inning of a game against the Cincinnati Redlegs, the left-handed-hitting Snider was in the on-deck circle, ready to face Bill Kennedy, a southpaw pitcher, with two runners on base and the Dodgers trailing 11–6. Alston decided a right-handed hitter would fare better against Kennedy so he had me pinch-hit for Duke. As he walked back to the dugout, Duke flung his bat in disgust. Unfortunately, I grounded out to the third baseman.

"I didn't think Duke was sore, but I don't give a damn," Alston said. "At that point, I didn't especially want a home run. I just wanted a hit to keep us going."[9]

In 1957, the Dodgers were in the first of a two-year youth movement that reshaped the franchise for the future.

John Roseboro was being groomed to succeed Roy Campanella at catcher.

Don Drysdale won seventeen games to replace Don Newcombe as the ace of the pitching staff. Koufax's won-loss record of 5–4 was unspectacular, but his 122 strikeouts in 104 innings were signs of the greatness to come.

In the infield, the versatility of Neal, Gilliam, and Zimmer provided both short-term relief and long-term comfort as veterans like Pee Wee and me battled injuries.

Gino Cimoli played all three outfield positions so veterans Snider, Furillo, and Sandy Amoros could take turns resting.

Overseeing this transition was Alston, the best of the six managers I played for in the majors.

Alston played only one game in the big leagues, but he knew the game inside out. He managed a team of stars but didn't take guff from anybody. One night two players were arguing in the shower. A bear of a man at six foot two and two hundred pounds, Walter stepped between them. He picked one up with his left arm and then the second player

Walter Alston, right, was the best of the six managers Ransom Jackson, left, played for in the majors. The respect players had for Alston is reflected in the Dodgers winning seven National League pennants and four World Series titles under his leadership. National Baseball Hall of Fame Library, Cooperstown, NY.

with his right arm. "We're not going to have this anymore," he said firmly before setting them back down. Neither player made a peep.

The players respected him. That's why the Dodgers won seven National League pennants and four World Series titles under his leadership.

Complicating matters for Alston in 1957 was the ongoing speculation that the Dodgers were leaving Brooklyn for greener pastures in Los Angeles. Dodger owner Walter O'Malley wanted a new, larger ballpark as Ebbets Field was the smallest in the majors. Just before spring training started, he turned up the heat on New York City officials by acquiring the territorial rights needed to play in L.A. The question wasn't whether the Dodgers would move but when.

In the next-to-last game of the season in Philadelphia against the Phillies, I hit a three-run homer into the upper-left-field deck at Connie Mack Stadium to help the Dodgers win 8–4. The home run didn't seem all that significant at the time, even though no other Dodger homered the rest of the game or the following day. We were in third place, well behind the pennant-winning Milwaukee Braves and second-place St. Louis Cardinals. Shortly after the season ended, the Dodgers made it official that they were going to L.A.

Some thirty years later my son Chuck called from his home in Columbus, Georgia, to tell me that I was the subject of a trivia question on the television show *Good Morning America.*

"They asked, 'Who was the last Brooklyn Dodger to hit a home run,'" Chuck said. "Dad, the answer was you!"

Only then did I realize the historical importance of my home run. It even earned me a spot in the Brooklyn Dodgers Hall of Fame—a nice consolation prize for a bummer of a season.

25

THE DAY THE MUSIC DIED

Brooklyn's Ebbets Fields was a fun place to work.

In the smallest ballpark in the major leagues with a seating capacity of approximately thirty-two thousand, the fans were so close I could almost shake hands with them from my third-base position.

The grandstand was filled with characters such as Hilda Chester, who rallied the crowd with a cowbell. Another fan used a police whistle.

There was organist Gladys Goodding playing the usual ballpark songs and a pep band that played the unusual, like "Three Blind Mice" when an umpire made a questionable call against the Dodgers. Band members dressed like bums and called themselves the "Dodger Symphony." The band was horrible but they made a lot of noise, creating a party atmosphere for the fans and making the games even more entertaining.

Only 6,702 fans showed up September 24, 1957, for what turned out to be the last game at Ebbets Field. Rookie Danny McDevitt pitched a five-hit shutout against the Pittsburgh Pirates, but Gladys stole the show on her Hammond organ with a repertoire of songs fit for a funeral.

It was widely speculated that the Dodgers were moving to Los Angeles after sixty-eight years in Brooklyn. But the official announcement didn't come until two weeks later—October 8.

Meanwhile, Gladys was on a mission of her own.

In addition to playing the organ at Ebbets Field and Madison Square Garden where the New York Knicks and New York Rangers played, she sang "The Star-Spangled Banner."

Gladys arrived at the ballpark for the final game carrying a little brown bag. She made a beeline for the booth where the organ was located, shut the door, and locked it.

"Gladys was known to have a drink or three once in a while," recalled Vin Scully, the Dodgers' fabled play-by-play announcer. "And the first song she played that night was 'My Buddy,' which is one of the saddest songs you'll ever want to hear. She went down from there."[1]

When the Dodgers scored in the first inning, Gladys responded with "After You're Gone," and "Am I Blue?"

Dodger owner Walter O'Malley pounded on the door, pleading, "Knock it off, Gladys."

Gladys couldn't be fired, so she banged out "Don't Ask Me Why I'm Leaving" after the Dodgers scored another run in the third inning.

I was listening to all this in the dugout as I didn't play in the game. Gladys delivered what Dodger historian Mark Langill calls "the musical boot out of town."

"I think she was taking a nip here and there as she played the organ," Scully said. "By the time the game was over, it was the most depressive night you'd ever experience."[2]

Gladys didn't miss a beat, playing "So Long, It's Been Good to Know You," "Que Sera Sera," "When I Grow Too Old to Dream," "Say It Isn't So," "If I Had My Way," "Thanks for the Memories," "May the Lord Bless You and Keep You," "Auld Lang Syne," and "What Can I Say Dear, after I Say I'm Sorry?"

The kicker was "California, Here I Come."

It was a virtuoso performance, one that expressed the feelings of Dodger fans that the world was ending.

Gladys spelled her last name G-O-O-D-D-I-N-G. "She always feared that when she passed away, her name would be misspelled in her obituary," Langill said.

Goodding died in 1963 at the age of seventy. A wire-service story in the Moberly, Missouri, *Monitor-Index* began, "dGlays [*sic*] Gooding. . . ."[3] By the end of the article, the newspaper got it right: "The Brooklyn Dodgers are no more—they went to Los Angeles. And Ebbets

Field has been torn down for a housing project. Even Madison Square Garden soon will move to a new location. And now Gladys Goodding."[4]

Even though I was there when the Dodgers left town, I didn't fully realize the traumatic effect it had on entire Brooklyn families until I got a handwritten letter a half century later from Jimmy Dunn, a lifelong Dodger fan. The letter begins:

> Dear Mr. Jackson:
> I was born a Dodger fan. Having a father born in Brooklyn, bedtime during my childhood consisted of Dodger tales, trivia and statistics. My grandparents' second date was a Dodger/Giant game at the Polo Grounds. They later raised a family in Bay Ridge and were neighbors of Pee Wee Reese. A number of my early life lessons were taught through Dodger lore: Pee Wee's arm around Jackie [Robinson]; [Sandy] Koufax's religious strength and the refusal to pitch on Yom Kippur; Vin Scully and Tommy Lasorda and the importance of loyalty. My Dad used to say that being a Dodger fan was like being Irish—you're born into it, you embrace it and grow with it.

Accompanying the letter were baseball cards showing me in a Dodger uniform. Jimmy continued:

> These Dodger baseball cards were eventually handed down to me. I have studied these cards over countless hours and the players and the images are not only a part of Dodger history but part of the history of my family. The last Brooklyn Dodger game my grandfather saw was [Don] Larsen's perfect game. The tickets were given to my grandfather by Carl Furillo's father-in-law. They both owned bars in Brooklyn. After the Dodgers left Brooklyn, my grandfather moved the family to Chicago. If there were no Dodgers in Brooklyn, there was no reason to stay, he'd tell me.
> My grandfather has since passed away and these Dodger stories along with the lessons I've learned still live on. I imagine my heaven to be like Field of Dreams. Instead of Iowa, however, it will be Brooklyn at Ebbets Field in the 1950s and my grandfather will be there to meet me with tickets to a World Series game.
> Mr. Jackson, I have included one of the many cards I've studied over the years in hopes you would be kind enough to sign it for me: To Jimmy, if possible. Your name was one of many I learned at an early age—Leo the Lip [Leo Durocher], Duke [Snider], Pee Wee,

Oisk [Carl Erskine], Newk [Don Newcombe] and Handsome Ransom. Thank you very much for your time, Mr. Jackson.

Reading Jimmy's letter, I'm reminded that it's really the Dodger players that should be thanking Brooklyn fans. The memories we gave them pale in comparison to those they gave us.

26

STAR WATCHING IN L.A.

The Brooklyn Dodger team that endeared itself to millions didn't move west to Los Angeles in 1958—their shadows did.

A car accident during the off-season left catcher Roy Campanella paralyzed for life. The other stars on the team who inspired the "Boys of Summer" nickname were well into the winter of their careers. Pee Wee Reese was thirty-nine; Carl Furillo, thirty-six; Gil Hodges, thirty-four; Don Newcombe, thirty-two; Duke Snider, Carl Erskine, and Clem Labine, all thirty-one.

The present was the future and the development of talented young prospects such as outfielders Ron Fairly, nineteen; Frank Howard, twenty-one; and Don Demeter, twenty-three; catcher John Roseboro, twenty-five; and pitchers Stan Williams, twenty-one, and Larry Sherry and Sandy Koufax, both twenty-two.

The building blocks of a great pitching staff already were in place. Don Drysdale, twenty-one, and Johnny Podres, twenty-five, were coming off outstanding seasons that saw them win seventeen and twelve games, respectively.

None of us knew for sure we were going to Los Angeles until the official announcement after the 1957 season ended. I was somewhat familiar with L.A. because I played briefly for the Angels of the old Pacific Coast League (PCL) in 1949. I didn't know the way to San Jose but I knew how to get to Catalina Island.

It looked like I might have more time to spend on Catalina. I was thirty-two and at a crossroads with the Dodgers.

Third base was as congested as an L.A. freeway with me vying for the starter's job with Dick Gray, a promising rookie, and Pee Wee, Jim "Junior" Gilliam, and Don Zimmer ready to jump in if we stumbled.

"When Jackson's hot, he swings a blazing bat, but he's one of those tough-luck guys who are prone to injuries of one sort or another," Frank Finch of the *Los Angeles Times* wrote in a story introducing me to local readers.[1]

Finch recounted my freakish injuries, concluding: "And this is the guy who went through three rugged Southwest Conference campaigns as a football star at Texas and TCU!"[2]

The biggest challenge in relocating to L.A. was our new ballpark. And that's really a misuse of the terms "new" and "ballpark."

The Los Angeles Memorial Coliseum was the site of the 1932 Olympic Games and primarily a track and football facility. The Los Angeles Rams of the National Football League played there as did the USC and UCLA football teams.

Nearby was a clone of Chicago's Wrigley Field. It also was named Wrigley Field and from 1925 through 1957 was the home of the PCL Angels. But the Coliseum seated more than one hundred thousand people and L.A.'s Wrigley only twenty-two thousand. That's fewer fans than Brooklyn's Ebbets Field seated, so owner Walter O'Malley wasn't going to settle for that. The Dodgers played four years at the Coliseum while a real ballpark, Dodger Stadium, was being built with private funding—the first since Yankee Stadium in 1923.

True to its name, the Coliseum was a colossus of a place for baseball. It was 440 feet from home plate to center field; 301 feet down the right-field line, and 251 feet to the left-field foul pole. A forty-foot net was erected in left field so the players weren't confused thinking they were on a Little League diamond.

When I saw the playing field for the first time, I thought to myself: "Weird, weird, weird."

San Francisco Giants pitcher Johnny Antonelli called the left-field screen "the biggest farce I ever heard of."[3]

Drysdale said the screen, dubbed the "Chinese Wall" by sportswriters, turned the game into a sideshow. "Who feels like playing baseball in this place?"[4]

Line drives that were sure homers elsewhere became singles or doubles when hit toward the screen. High fly ball outs were home runs called "Moon shots" after Wally Moon joined the Dodgers in 1959 and made an art of lofting towering flies over the screen.

The right-field fence cut across the middle of the football field. It was Death Valley for left-handed hitters like Snider who watched 400-foot blasts to right center die and be caught for outs.

"Duke, they killed you," the Giants' Willie Mays said to Snider. "Man, they took the bat right out of your hands."[5]

Duke went from five straight seasons of forty-plus homers to fifteen, only six at the Coliseum.

The best part about playing in the Coliseum was the huge crowds. Attendance skyrocketed to more than 1.8 million, almost double our last season in Brooklyn.

One fan created his own version of Ebbets Field's pep band with bugle calls that the crowd answered with cries of "C-H-A-R-G-E!" It wasn't long before the Dodgers had their own bugle corps, hundreds of fans leading charges with foot-long brass bugles purchased for a dollar at Coliseum concession stands.

The Coliseum was lousy for watching baseball.

"In the far reaches of the vast arena the game resembled a pantomime," Al Wolf of the *L.A. Times* reported after an opening day crowd of 78,672—a National League record. "You couldn't follow the ball, but the actions of the players told you what was happening. Nobody complained."[6]

Instead of complaining, they started bringing transistor radios to the games so Dodger play-by-play announcers Vin Scully and Jerry Doggett could tell them what was happening on the field.

Some of the fans were Hollywood celebrities.

The biggest television and movie stars of the era showed up—Dean Martin, Jerry Lewis, Cary Grant, Jimmy Stewart, Burt Lancaster, Danny Kaye, Nat King Cole, Dinah Shore, Edward G. Robinson, Bing Crosby, Jack Benny, and Bob Hope, to name a few.

Comedian Milton Berle had box seats near the Dodger dugout for his wife and friends such as Jack Lemmon, Walter Matthau, and Neil Simon.

Groucho Marx was there with his cigar and Gene Autry with his cowboy hat.

"Ballplayers want to be stars and stars want to be ballplayers," Dodger historian Mark Langill explained.

Star watching was a favorite sport among the players. Rather than follow the game, we gazed for stars in the stands.

"What's the score?"

"I don't know. But look, there's so-and-so."

"Oh, yeah!"

Erskine was pitching one game when he glanced over at the dugout and saw several guys with "their necks craned . . . gawking into the stands at Lana Turner."[7]

Spotting glamorous women like Turner was more fun than being one of the fading stars on the field.

The Dodgers used eight different players at third base in 1958, including Gil Hodges, a first baseman. I started only fourteen games at third—one more than Gil. Gray got the most starts (fifty-three), followed by the versatile Gilliam (thirty-nine).

Every team seems to have one position that is a problem child.

The Chicago Cubs, for example, have searched in vain for a steady performer in center field since 1951 when they traded Andy Pafko, a four-time All-Star, to Brooklyn.

For the Dodgers, third base has lived up to its reputation as the hot corner.

Jackie Robinson, primarily a second baseman, replaced slick-fielding Billy Cox in 1955 because the Dodgers needed more firepower at the position.

From 1958 until 1972, forty-three players were tried at third. The list is a Who's Who of baseball in the 1960s: Roseboro, a catcher; outfielder Tommy Davis; shortstop Maury Wills; and first basemen Bill Skowron, Dick Allen, and Steve Garvey. Not even Ken Boyer, a seventime All-Star at third, could hold the job for long. Finally, Ron Cey arrived in 1972 to give the Dodgers a decade of stability at the position.

Drysdale best summed up 1958 when he called it "one totally screwed-up season . . . a wasted summer."[8]

The Dodgers even finished one game behind the Cubs with a 71–83 record, seventh in an eight-team league. The Cubs tied for fifth place.

I was batting .185 when I was sold to the Cleveland Indians in early August. I was healthy and anxious to play again, but I was going to miss the star watching in L.A. In Cleveland, there were no movie stars to watch. Bob Hope, the city's adopted son and most famous star, left for L.A. long before the Dodgers.

Third base lived up to its nickname as the "hot corner" in 1958 for the Los Angeles Dodgers as Ransom Jackson was one of eight players to see action at the position. Courtesy Los Angeles Dodgers.

27

DETOUR TO CLEVELAND

Frank Lane was nicknamed "Trader Frank" because of the four hundred–plus deals he made as general manager for six major-league teams. I was involved in two of them—one that brought me to the Cleveland Indians in August 1958 and the other that sent me away the following May.

Joe Gordon was the Indians' manager and Rocky Colavito its star player when I arrived in Cleveland. Both wound up being traded to the Detroit Tigers. If given the chance, Trader Frank would've swapped his mother.

Going to Cleveland was a chance to play every day, something I hadn't done since leaving the Chicago Cubs in 1955.

"We needed a third baseman and Jackson fills the bill," Lane said of the deal that cost the Indians $20,000. "He's a good glove man and if played regularly should bat .275."[1]

Gordon was happy, calling the acquisition a big steal.

"I know Frank has made some great deals in his time," Gordon said, "and this Jackson purchase, I'm convinced, eventually will be listed as one of his best."[2]

I was stale from sitting on the bench in L.A. The first time I batted in my first start for the Indians, I ripped a ball over the center fielder's head for a triple. As I was running from second to third, I pulled a leg muscle. That sidelined me until nearly two weeks later when we played the Boston Red Sox in a three-game series at Fenway Park.

I had never seen the Red Sox's Ted Williams play. He was called "The Splendid Splinter" because he's regarded by many to be the greatest hitter to ever live. So I went to the dugout early to sit and watch him take batting practice. For twenty minutes I watched Ted put on a hitting clinic, truly a splendid sight.

I was still sitting on the bench in the ninth inning of the first game when Gordon walked up to me and said, "You're pinch-hitting."

I did my best imitation of Ted, belting a pitch from Boston's Tom Brewer over the Green Monster in left field for a home run.

The next day Gordon said, "You're starting."

It was my second start for the Indians and first since I was injured. When Ted, a left-handed pull hitter, came to bat in the first inning, the entire infield shifted several feet to the right. This put me where the shortstop usually plays. I was standing there thinking, "Here I am after all these years playing against Ted Williams. It's great to be alive."

Another thought I had while daydreaming was: "The ball won't come to me because Ted always hits to right field."

Ted swung and the ball shot toward me. I was almost frozen, unable to react in time to the ball taking one hop and rocketing off the shin of my right knee. Ted was given a well-deserved hit on the play. I got a nasty bruise and knot and a memory of Ted Williams that has lasted a lifetime. It made the detour to Cleveland worthwhile.

28

BACK WHERE I STARTED

News of my return to the Chicago Cubs in 1959 was as surprising as the announcement in 1955 that I was leaving in a trade to the Brooklyn Dodgers. I was just as happy to be back with the Cubs as I was when I left. It was a homecoming.

The Dodgers gave me a chance to play on a championship team and in the World Series. Rejoining the Cubs was an opportunity to finish my career in a ballpark I loved.

I loved playing in the daylight because I hit better.

I loved having evenings free to be at home with my family.

I loved the ivy-covered brick walls in the outfield.

Most of all, I loved the fans. In the fifties, there weren't as many of them as there are today, but they were no less passionate and loyal. At the time, fans were allowed to come down to the box seats near the field during batting practice. I made it a point to walk over and talk with them.

The Cubs acquired me from Cleveland for the same reason the Dodgers did four years earlier. I was insurance in case the legs buckled on Alvin Dark, the Cubs' starting third baseman. He was thirty-seven years old, the same age as Jackie Robinson when I joined the Dodgers.

The season was nearly a month old when I reported to the Cubs.

The uniform number two I had always worn now belonged to out-fielder Lee Walls. So Yosh Kawano, the Cubs' equipment manager, gave me number twenty-two.

"Double or nothing," Yosh said.

"I'll settle for singles," I replied.

I appeared in twenty-nine games for Cleveland in 1958, hitting .242. I was in only three games in 1959 before "Trader" Frank Lane dispatched me to Chicago.

The Cubs had a different manager, Bob Scheffing, and general manager, John Holland, but the results on the field were practically the same. They finished fifth among eight teams the year before and would do it again in 1959.

Ernie Banks was at the top of his game, winning the National League Most Valuable Player Award both years, and Tony Taylor was starting to make a name for himself at second base, but the other stars on the team were past their prime. Besides Dark, there were outfielders Bobby Thomson, age thirty-five, and Walt Moryn, thirty-three; and first baseman Dale Long, thirty-three. The last month of the season a twenty-one-year-old outfielder named Billy Williams made his big-league debut. He went on to become one of the all-time Cub greats.

Dark was healthy and playing regularly so I kept busy throwing batting practice to the pitchers. I grooved the ball down the middle and they'd swing real hard. It made them feel like hitters; I felt like a pitcher. That was better than feeling like a benchwarmer.

When I started a game, it was a surprise. After pitching batting practice for forty-five minutes, I'd walk into the dugout to see my name posted on the lineup card.

There were a few moments of glory.

My first week back with the Cubs I tripled in the tying and winning runs in the tenth inning to beat the St. Louis Cardinals and then socked a three-run homer to put us ahead of the Cards in another game that we eventually lost.

You've got to play to produce. I wasn't playing or contributing much with one homer and a .241 batting average for my last forty-one games in a Cub uniform. Baseball always was a job, but it also was a game that once was a lot of fun. The fun was gone; it was now just another job.

I made up my mind to retire weeks before the season ended against the Los Angeles Dodgers at Wrigley Field.

My last at bat on September 25, 1959, involved Don Drysdale, my ex-roommate; Williams, a future Hall of Famer, and Danny McDevitt, the winning pitcher in the Dodgers' last game at Ebbets Field in Brooklyn.

One of Ransom Jackson's teammates when he returned to the Chicago Cubs in 1959 was Bobby Thomson, infamous among Dodger fans for the home run he hit to beat Brooklyn in the 1951 National League playoff. Left to right are Thomson; first baseman Jim Marshall; Jackson; and catcher Cal Neeman. Ransom Jackson Collection.

We were one run down with a runner on first with nobody out in the seventh inning when Williams, a left-hander, walked to the plate to bat against Drysdale, a right-hander. The Dodgers countered by bringing in McDevitt, a southpaw. I bat from the right side, so I pinch-hit for Williams, also a pinch hitter.

I had visions of a repeat of 1954 when I blasted the ball five hundred feet over the left-field bleachers and Waveland Avenue, crashing into the third floor of an apartment building. Then I looked toward the third-base coach. He flashed the bunt signal. If I was looking for a sign to retire, that was it.

I bunted, advancing the runner to second. I was safe at first on a throwing error and then replaced unceremoniously by a pinch runner. That was it. No game-winning, tape-measure homer. A sacrifice bunt in my last of 3,549 plate appearances is how it ended. The Dodgers won 5–4 in eleven innings.

I watched the final two games from the dugout as the Dodgers won on the last day of the season to finish in a first-place tie with the Milwaukee Braves. They beat the Braves in a playoff and the Chicago White Sox in the World Series.

Shortly after L.A. traded me to Cleveland the year before, a wire-service reporter asked me about the Dodgers' future.

"Frankly, I don't think the Dodgers will win the pennant again for a number of years to come," I said. "Not until a lot of their younger players start to establish themselves, anyway."[1]

That pretty much doomed me as a sports prognosticator.

After the last game I walked into Holland's office to let him know of my decision. "I will not be back next year," I said. "Good luck."

The headline of a story in the *Chicago American* read: RANDY JACKSON QUITS BASEBALL; EXITS LAUGHING.[2]

That really wasn't the case, but I probably had a smirk on my face the next day when the Cubs announced they were replacing Scheffing, the team's most successful manager in the 1950s, with Charlie Grimm, a manager they had already fired twice. In fact, Charlie was at the helm for my first spring training in 1948. "The more things change, the more they remain the same," I thought to myself.

Charlie lasted seventeen games into the 1960 season when the Cubs raised even more eyebrows, this one producing a laugh. They traded Charlie to radio station WGN for color commentator Lou Boudreau, a former player and manager. Charlie remained a Cub vice president in case he was needed to manage the team again.

Other teams built for the future; the Cubs dwelled in the past. I never looked back as I drove home to Athens, Georgia.

During the World Series between the Dodgers and the White Sox, a Chicago sportswriter asked Drysdale about my pending retirement. "When the weather warms up next spring," Don said, "and everybody is itching to get going again, maybe Randy will have a change of heart and get back in uniform."[3]

When told of Don's remark, I said: "Tell Don when I get that kind of an itch I'll head for the golf course instead. I'm quitting baseball for keeps."[4]

Part 3

Life after Baseball

29

WHERE CAN YOU GO FROM THERE?

Ben Howard "Rosie" Cantrell played for the Travelers, the minor-league baseball team in my hometown of Little Rock, Arkansas, for five seasons in the 1940s. Rosie had a reputation for hitting the bottle as hard as the ball. He had a .315 career batting average in almost two thousand games to prove it.

Rosie was shagging fly balls in the outfield before one game in Little Rock when teammate Marland "Duke" Doolittle walked up to him.

"Rosie, why don't you quit drinking?" Duke asked. "You're such a good hitter that you'd go to the big leagues in nothing flat if they knew you weren't messing around with liquor anymore."

Rosie thought about the question for a moment. "Why would I want to do that?" he said. "Where can you go from there?"

I was asking the same question after the 1959 season when I told the Chicago Cubs I was quitting baseball, giving up a yearly salary of $21,000. In 2015 dollars, that's roughly $171,000.

I was nearly thirty-four with a wife, two kids, a mortgage, and no job.

My college diploma was covered with dust. I had experience running a laundry business with my parents, but it folded like a newly pressed pair of pants two years after we bought it.

Everything I had done in my life had pretty much been decided for me.

The world was at war in 1944 when I turned eighteen. It was a foregone conclusion I was going into the military. The only decision was what uniform I was going to wear. Once I entered pro baseball in 1948, my career path was determined by the teams that owned my contract. I had no control over where I was going to play.

I was at a party when John Bailey, a friend of my wife, Ruth, asked what I planned on doing now that I was out of baseball.

"I'm open to ideas," I said.

John invited me to Atlanta so he could introduce me to a group of people starting a new company, Georgia International Life Insurance. Three months earlier they had invested $10 million worth of stock in the company and it sold out the first day on the market.

I sold insurance one winter in Chicago. That was when the Cubs traded me to Brooklyn, explaining they needed a holler guy to liven up the team's infield play. "Holler guys don't sell insurance to important people," I said.

That's all I knew about selling insurance.

Dad made a decent living as an insurance salesman during the Depression. Maybe this was the answer to Rosie's question, "Where can you go from there?"

I went to Atlanta; met the company's fifteen employees, including the president; and listened carefully to John's pitch.

"We're not big enough to train you so you'll have to teach yourself," John said.

That was fine by me. I taught myself how to hit even though the Cubs had Rogers Hornsby as a hitting instructor. He never said one word to me; he was too busy handicapping the horses at Arlington Park, a racetrack in the Chicago area.

"The company has great products and the future is bright," John continued.

He sold life insurance for New York Life before joining Georgia International as head recruiter.

"Not only will you make a commission but every year you'll get some stock options."

Not even Mickey Mantle got stock options with the New York Yankees. I signed up.

It was the best decision I ever made. I sold enough insurance to qualify for trips to sales events all over the United States, the Caribbean, and Europe. Everything was first class.

Georgia International expanded throughout the U.S. and into Puerto Rico. Eventually, it was acquired by a British company and later another U.S. firm.

Rosie Cantrell never made it to the Big Show. He preferred staying in the minors where he didn't have to deal with the question "Where can you go from there?"

I got lucky again. John Bailey answered that question for me.

30

I'M NO JOE

Joe Garagiola is best known as a witty sportscaster and one of the hosts on NBC television's *Today Show* for many years. He came to the Chicago Cubs in the 1953 megatrade for Ralph Kiner. That's how I got to know Joe.

He was a good defensive catcher and a better hitter than the self-deprecating stories he liked to tell on TV. Joe was a motormouth, but nobody cared because he was such a funny guy with a gift for making people laugh. Joe's quick wit made him a natural in the broadcast booth. But near the end of his playing days Cub announcer Jack Brickhouse advised him "to stay with some phase of baseball and forget broadcasting."[1]

Years later Joe reminded Brickhouse of this on the air. "Jack, before you start questioning me, I understand you told Edison to forget the light bulb and Eli Whitney to forget the cotton gin—that the chances of success were slim."[2]

Brickhouse didn't bother saying anything to me about broadcasting.

When I left baseball in 1959, there were not very many ex-athletes or "jocks" in the broadcast business.

The most famous was Dizzy Dean, the Hall of Fame pitcher who mangled the English language as a commentator on *Game of the Week* for CBS television. Dizzy said "slud" instead of "slid" and regularly used "ain't."

Dizzy once received a letter from an English teacher, lamenting the poor example he was setting for kids. "A lot of folks who ain't sayin' 'ain't,' ain't eatin',"Dizzy lectured on the next telecast. "So, Teach, you learn 'em English, and I'll learn 'em baseball."

I wasn't as fast with the one-liners as Dizzy or Joe. But this didn't stop me from accepting an invitation from Ed Thilenius, a friend and longtime University of Georgia football announcer, to be his sidekick on the telecasts of twenty Atlanta Crackers home games during the 1962 and 1963 seasons.

I was paid one hundred dollars a game, driving back and forth to Atlanta from my home in Athens, Georgia, for each game, a round-trip of about 150 miles.

Using the knowledge and insights gained from playing ten years in the majors, my job was to provide color commentary that would make the games more entertaining to Cracker fans watching on WAGA-TV in Atlanta. I was an experienced public speaker and I enjoy telling stories, especially about baseball. This was going to be fun.

And it was. The Crackers were members of the International League and one of their stars in 1962 was Tim McCarver, a catcher who went on to become an outstanding announcer. Thilenius was an old pro, as comfortable in front of a camera as he was chatting by the fireplace. He made it easy for me.

"What do you think of that, Randy?"

"He hit that ball pretty good."

"That was a close play at third, Randy."

"They don't get much closer, Ed."

I was no Joe Garagiola, but it didn't matter much until the day Ed wasn't in the broadcast booth when the game was about to begin and the light on the camera came on, indicating we were on the air.

As part of his pregame preparation, Ed talked with the players on the field of Ponce de Leon Park, gathering information he could share with viewers. I stayed in the booth and penciled the lineups in the scorebook so it was ready when Ed returned about fifteen minutes before the game started.

Ed wasn't around and the camera was running. I wasn't going to sing "Wabash Cannonball" like Dizzy used to do. I had appeared on the nationally televised *Ed Sullivan Show* with my Brooklyn Dodger teammates just before the 1956 World Series, but it wasn't a speaking role.

"Hello there, I'm Randy Jackson," I began. "Nice that you could join us for tonight's game."

I was talking to a million-plus people across Georgia and parts of Alabama and Tennessee and didn't have anything to say. Sweat was pouring off of me. Where's Ed when I need him the most?

Finally, Ed showed up. The door to the booth was locked and he had to find somebody to unlock it for him.

Seeing that camera light come on was as frightening as the two times in the minors I got hit in the head. The experience also gave me a greater appreciation for former players like Garagiola, McCarver, Bob Uecker, Ernie Johnson, Joe Morgan, Orel Hershiser, and many others who became accomplished broadcasters.

Sportscaster Howard Cosell derided jocks, saying all they brought to the broadcast booth was mediocrity. "I can't quarrel with that because if there's an expert on mediocrity, it is Cosell," Garagiola quipped.[3]

There wasn't a future for me in broadcasting, but there's one for ex-pitchers like John Smoltz and Tom Glavine working alongside professional announcers.

"You look at the grass and you see it's manicured beautifully and you describe it so well," Garagiola told Brickhouse in an interview. "I look at it and I say, 'If I'm not careful that ball is gonna skip off that grass.'

"You look at the foul lines and you say the ground crew really did a great job and you build this beautiful word picture. I look at it and I say, 'Those sonofaguns, they tilted the foul lines and that ball is gonna stay fair. . . .'"[4]

Joe nailed it. My broadcast partner, Ed Thilenius, looked at the camera light and knew exactly what to say. I looked at the same light when I was alone that one time and all I could say was, "Where's Ed?"

31

MY FRIEND, DAD

We shared a lot more than our names, Ransom Joseph. We were navy men, golf buddies, and business partners. We played the same position in baseball—third base. He meticulously prepared scrapbooks with newspaper articles covering my sports career. We even took piano lessons together.

Everybody in the family was going to learn how to play the piano—Mom, Dad, me, and my sister, Suzanne.

Our teacher was a family friend named Jimmy. The first Tuesday of every month he came to our house in Little Rock, Arkansas, with a bag of Hershey's Kisses candy for us and our terrier, Little Bits.

Jimmy used just the chords and the melody of the music to teach. It was much easier than the traditional way piano is taught.

The lessons turned out to be like musical chairs. Mom quit after two months. Dad and Suzanne stopped a month later. This left me alone on the piano bench.

I loved everything about playing the piano except for one thing. When my folks had a party, they would go with their friends to sit in the living room. I would be in my room studying and hear this sweet voice holler down the hall, "Ransom Junior!"

The show was on. I went to the living room and played whatever song that was popular at the time.

Dad subscribed to the newspapers wherever I played baseball so he could follow my games and then clip and paste stories about them in scrapbooks. "Ransom is going to have a full-time job just keeping up with the newspaper clippings," the *Princeton Alumni Weekly* reported in 1948 after I signed with the Chicago Cubs.[1]

Dad filled about a dozen scrapbooks that stir up old memories and keep me honest as a storyteller.

Sometimes Dad served as my spokesman.

When the Cubs named Stan Hack as manager in 1954, Dad told the sports columnist at the newspaper in Lawton, Oklahoma, where he was running our laundry business: "Don't quote me on anything to do with the managerial change at Chicago, but you can say that Randy respects Hack. In fact, the boy told me not too long ago that Hack has showed him everything he knows about playing third base."[2]

In another story, Dad lamented my not playing sports until I got to college. "I just badgered him so much about going out for sports at school that he eventually did it just to keep me quiet. At that, it took me five years before I won out."[3]

In a scrapbook covering the 1949 season, there's a photo of Mom and Dad sitting in the stands of the Oklahoma City ballpark. It was a Friday night but they were dressed in their finest Sunday clothes.

When I got to the majors, they came to see me play at Wrigley Field, signing autographs for fans recognizing the well-dressed couple as my parents. "They saw him play in two Cotton Bowl games," one writer reported. "Their goal now is to watch him in a World Series."[4]

The same story quotes me as saying, "My father has been a constant source of inspiration, never letting me get down when things get rough."[5]

Dad encouraged me with telegrams like this: CONGRATULATIONS ON YOUR GRAND SLAM. KNEW YOU COULD DO IT. REPEAT IT TOMORROW FOR US—MOTHER AND DAD; WILLIE AND HUGH.

We bantered with each other.

My first year as a pro with Des Moines in 1948, I sent Dad a telegram reading: GOT FOUR FOR FIVE TONIGHT. ARE YOU HAPPY?—RANSOM.

Dad taught me how to play golf, and he helped get me into the U.S. Navy's college training program that led to playing football and baseball at Texas Christian University and the University of Texas and, ultimately, in the major leagues.

Ransom and Ann Jackson could be found in the grandstands wherever their son, Ransom, was playing. This photo was taken at Oklahoma City's Holland Park in 1949 when young Ransom played for the Oklahoma City Indians, a Texas League team. Ransom Jackson Collection.

Dad also shared his knowledge and wisdom with the young cadets he was in charge of at Papa Jackson's Country Club. That was the nickname of the flight school he ran for the navy in Corpus Christi, Texas, during World War II. If the cadets had problems, Dad was their counselor. If they got into trouble, he stood up for them. Dad was affectionately called Papa Jackson.

On my first leave in the navy in December 1944, Dad sent a pilot in an open-air training plane to pick me up in Fort Worth and fly back to Corpus Christi. We were to meet at twelve noon sharp at the Fort Worth airport. Around one o'clock, the pilot stormed into the room and said, "I'm looking for Seaman Jackson."

I was in the wrong part of the airport, and he was visibly upset. This was confirmed when he removed his earplugs on landing in Corpus

Christi three and a half hours later. He gave me a helmet for the flight but no earplugs.

Dad invited me to join him and three other officers for their regularly scheduled poker night. My first hand was four kings and a jack. When the dealer asked if I wanted other cards, I politely said, "No, thanks."

After a few small bets were placed, everybody laid down their cards. Of course, I won. As I gathered the pot of four dollars, I looked up at the officers and could swear there was smoke coming out of their ears. I decided it was time for this lowly seaman to excuse himself and spend the rest of his evening with his mother.

I was home in Athens, Georgia, in late 1956 when Dad telephoned to say he was shutting down the laundry and dry cleaning business in Lawton.

The previous owner told Dad the business would thrive when groups of about two thousand U.S. army reservists arrived at nearby Fort Sill each month during the summer. It never happened. The army stopped sending reserves the first summer. Sales dropped immediately.

Dad was going to file for bankruptcy, but his accountants recommended paying the $6,000 owed in taxes and dissolve the business. That was the exact amount of money I received for playing in the 1956 World Series. I remembered Dad using all the money he had after the infamous 1929 stock market crash to pay off the debts of his brother and brother-in-law. I did the same for Dad; I cried as I wrote the check.

On December 6, 1969, Dad and I were watching "The Game of the Century" on television—Texas against Arkansas, both undefeated and ranked one-two in college football. I was in Athens; Dad was in Baton Rouge, Louisiana. Mom and Dad moved there near my sister, Suzanne, after closing the laundry business.

I got a call from Suzanne telling me Dad had a heart attack watching the game and was dead. Mom was supposed to play bridge at a neighbor's house but decided to stay home instead. I was glad she did because she knew immediately nothing could be done to help Dad. He was sixty-eight.

I flew to Baton Rouge with my two sons, Randy and Chuck, then thirteen and fourteen. At one point during the flight Chuck stared out the airplane window, looked back at me, and said, "Where's God?"

I didn't know what to say.

Today, I can imagine God together with Dad and Ernie Banks, talking about the virtues of patience. Ernie displayed the patience of Job with the Cubs. He didn't play on a winner until 1963, ten years after he joined the team. In his nineteen seasons with the Cubs, they finished no higher than second and never made it to the playoffs. The Cubs haven't been to a World Series since 1945, and the last one they won was in 1908. The eternal optimist, Ernie once said, "Good things come to those who wait and wait and wait."

Ernie was eight days shy of his eighty-fourth birthday and still waiting when he died in 2015.

In their conversation about patience, Ernie likely told God and Dad about the question on a T-shirt worn by a fan at Wrigley Field: "What did Jesus say to the Cubs?"

I can hear the three of them laughing at the answer: "Don't do nothin' 'til I get back."

32

THE LADY IN THE YELLOW TENNIS DRESS

The lifestyle of a baseball player puts a lot of strain on a marriage, from the pressure to excel and win to the constant travel for half the year to the inevitable injuries and trades. When the crowds stop cheering, the stress and uncertainty is different but it doesn't go away.

In 1968 my sixteen-year marriage to Ruth ended in divorce. Ruth got the house in Athens, Georgia, and custody of Randy, Chuck, and our daughter, Ann, who was born in 1964. I moved into a one-bedroom apartment near the Athens Country Club. All I took with me was my clothes, golf clubs, and a television.

I began karate lessons to get some consistent exercise. The teacher was a former army ranger and second-degree black belt. Every week for about two years I worked out with a bunch of guys about half my age in a building with no air-conditioning. I went from a white belt, the bottom of karate's colored belt system, to a brown belt.

"You're ready to get a black belt," the instructor said.

"Great, what do I do? Take some more tests?"

"No, you've got to fight. We'll go out of town and fight some guys."

"What? You mean, I've got to fight these young kids in their twenties just to get a black belt?"

"That's the way it's got to be done."

"Thank you very much," I said. "I'll just keep my leather belt that keeps my pants up."

That ended my karate career.

Meanwhile, the kids stayed with me every other weekend, sleeping on mattresses placed on the floor. We snacked on goodies, played games in a huge yard behind the apartment, and went to a lot of movies. The only one I remember is *Fantasia* because I slept through most of them.

By 1972, the boys were seventeen and eighteen and too big for this arrangement, but Ann, then eight, continued to come over on weekends.

One Saturday morning I went to pick up Ann at a friend's house where she spent the night. I knocked on the door. The woman opening it was wearing a yellow tennis dress and a hair dryer bonnet with the hose connected.

I found out she was a tennis instructor at Athens Country Club, so after playing golf one day, I stopped by the tennis courts. She was playing against a married couple I knew, and one of them invited me to join them. That's how I met Terry Yeargan.

Terry had just completed her master's degree in education at the University of Georgia and accepted a teaching position at a high school in Athens. She taught tennis during the summer. Her father, Percy "Skip" Yeargan, played baseball, football, and basketball in college and was head of the university's accounting department. She had two girls from a previous marriage—Meredith, three, and Ginny, who was eight and one of my daughter's classmates at school.

This gave me the brilliant idea of asking Terry if she'd give Ann tennis lessons in exchange for dinner one evening.

"I'll have to get a babysitter," she said. "Can you call me back?"

Terry called a friend, Barbara Dooley. "What do you know about this man? Should I go or not?"

"He's a great person," Barbara said. "He'd be good for you to date because he doesn't want to get married, either."

We started dating. I first introduced myself as Randy, so that's what she called me. After several dates I said, "My good friends call me Ransom."

"Okay, Randy," she said. Soon afterward she began calling me Ransom.

We got married September 1, 1972, but we didn't go on our honeymoon that weekend. I was scheduled to travel to England the following

April for a company convention. We made that our honeymoon, and I played in a golf tournament instead. Terry was my caddy.

Soon after we got married, we leased a single-engine airplane with two other couples and started taking flying lessons. The teacher always fussed at me while we were flying around.

"You turn it too fast. You've got to slow down. Da-da-da-da-da-da."

I did a series of landings one day and after the last one, he got out of the plane and said, "Take it up."

I took off and made four touch-and-go landings.

"How'd I do?" I asked as I got out of the plane.

"You did good."

"Let me tell you something," I said. "It's a whole lot better up there without you than it is with you."

That ended my aviation career. Terry kept her mouth shut and continued flying until she became pregnant in 1977 with our youngest son, Ransom Baxter.

Terry never saw me play baseball, so I was eager for her to meet my former Dodger teammates at reunions. At one of them, Chuck Connors, the ballplayer turned Rifleman on TV, gave her a big hug. Sandy Koufax kissed her on the cheek.

The Dodgers were a family in Brooklyn and, for the most part, they've maintained that tradition in Los Angeles, recognizing the contributions of ex-Dodgers.

A reunion in 1977 honored the Dodger and Giant teams that played the first major-league game on the West Coast in 1958. I strutted around the entire time because Terry was pregnant.

The highlight of a reunion in 1984 was a pregame ceremony retiring the jersey numbers worn by Pee Wee Reese and Don Drysdale. As I entered an inner concourse looking for the locker room, Koufax was standing there. We shook hands and spoke, and he directed me to an elderly man to usher me the rest of the way. I was still in street clothes sitting by my locker when Connors sauntered in, nodded politely, and started dressing next to me. Nothing was said until I finished putting on my uniform. "Randy, great to see you!" Chuck said, standing up to grab my hand. He didn't recognize me out of uniform any more than I did the gentleman who showed me to the locker room—actor Danny Kaye.

In 2008 the Dodgers celebrated their fiftieth anniversary in L.A. with an exhibition game against the Boston Red Sox before a record

Chuck Connors, best known as the star of the popular television series *The Rifle-man*, had trouble recognizing Ransom Jackson at one of the Dodger reunions but no problems making friends with Terry Jackson, "the lady in the yellow tennis dress" whom Ransom married in 1972. Ransom Jackson Collection.

crowd of 115,300 at the Los Angeles Memorial Coliseum. As awful a place as the Coliseum was for baseball, it was awesome to see that many people at a baseball game.

One of the first players to greet me was Dick Gray. We hadn't seen each other since 1958 when he was being groomed to take my place at third base. "What's new, Ransom?" he said, picking up where we'd left off a half century earlier.

The celebration continued at Dodger Stadium on Opening Day with a pregame ceremony right out of the movie *Field of Dreams*.

Duke Snider, wearing his Brooklyn Dodger uniform, appeared from the outfield bullpen and walked to his old position in center field. The procession of ex-Dodgers went on for fifteen minutes. I walked to third base with Gray, Ken McMullen, and Ron Cey; Maury Wills and Bill Russell to shortstop; Steve Sax to second, Eric Karros to first—forty players representing the different eras of the Dodgers' wonderful past. The showstopper was when Koufax, Don Newcombe, and Carl Erskine, three of the greatest pitchers to wear a Dodger uniform, appeared on the pitching mound and together threw out the first pitch.

Four former Los Angeles Dodger third basemen took the field at Dodger Stadium in 2008 to celebrate the team's fiftieth anniversary in L.A. Left to right: Ken McMullen, Ransom Jackson, Ron Cey, and Dick Gray. Courtesy Jon SooHoo / Los Angeles Dodgers LLC.

It was a poignant moment, one that reminded me of teammates like Drysdale who were not there. Don, my twenty-year-old roomie on the Dodgers' 1956 tour of Japan, died in 1993 at the age of fifty-six.

Reunions like this connect the past and the present to give both greater meaning. Terry never saw me play, but seeing me on the field with so many Dodger greats gave her a glimpse of what it was like at Ebbets Field in Brooklyn.

She also got to experience what it was like at Yankee Stadium in the 1956 World Series when Don Larsen of the New York Yankees pitched a perfect game against the Dodgers. To mark the thirty-fifth anniversary in 1991, the two teams gathered as many players as possible from the original game to play two innings. The sequel was better. I didn't play in the 1956 game, but this time I walked against Whitey Ford in my only at bat.

That evening we had dinner on the club level of Yankee Stadium. A band was playing music. Terry felt a tap on her shoulder. She looked up to see Yogi Berra. He asked her to dance.

When we got back to the hotel around one o'clock in the morning Terry phoned her father, then living in Alabama. "Guess who I just danced with?" she said excitedly. "Yogi Berra."

The dance with Yogi gave Terry a memory for a lifetime just as seeing her in a yellow tennis dress was the moment that changed my life.

33

MY FIRST LOVE

There's no explaining some things in life. I didn't play football or baseball in high school, but I played both in college as well as major-league baseball. I played golf in high school but not in college. The irony is that golf was my first love.

I started playing golf when I was twelve years old. Dad was an outstanding golfer and a member of the Little Rock Country Club. I spent summers on the fairways there, playing from eight o'clock in the morning until six at night. Another place I could be found was an empty lot next door to our house in Little Rock that neighborhood kids used as a putt-putt golf course.

Golf was something I could do on my own or with Dad. He got me interested in golf and gave me the coaching needed to get better.

Dad was a scratch golfer—someone who can play to a course handicap of zero. My lowest handicap was two, the highest twelve. When I gave up golf at age eighty-two, my handicap was ten.

In the fifties, baseball teams generally frowned on players golfing. In fact, Luke Sewell, manager of the Cincinnati Redlegs from 1950 to 1952, banned golf during spring training. He believed a pitcher's shoulder muscles could stiffen from swinging golf clubs and walking eighteen holes could cause leg muscles to tighten. "I've seen players shirk baseball to save themselves for golf," Sewell explained.[1]

Swinging a golf club and bat are polar opposites, the argument went, and golf messes up a hitter's natural swing.

"The swings are as far apart as they could be and still go by the same name," said Stan "The Man" Musial, one of baseball's all-time great hitters. "You never see a good golfer—Ben Hogan, for example—take an afternoon off to play a friendly game of baseball."[2]

In 1951, a nationally syndicated story on the subject pointed out that movies of the swings of Joe DiMaggio and a professional golfer were almost identical.

"The games require the same type of coordination," said Gene Sarazen, one of the world's top golfers in the 1920s and 1930s.[3]

Most baseball people didn't share this view. Teams wanting to pressure a player publicly sometimes used hometown sportswriters as messengers.

The fluctuation of my batting average from .275 in 1951 to .232 in 1952 to .285 in 1953 made me a perfect target for those believing golf and baseball don't mix.

One writer questioned how anybody could shoot in the low seventies and still focus on baseball.

In early 1954, the *Chicago American* published a story headlined: RANDY QUITS GOLF, FINDS IT HURTS HIS HITTING.[4]

"After a study of his batting averages over the past three seasons," the article read, "Jackson has decided to give up golf, aside from an occasional round for recreation and fellowship."[5]

According to the writer, my hitting woes in 1952 resulted from being "really bitten by this golf bug" and playing "whenever an opportunity presented itself." The explanation for my comeback in 1953 was "Randy tossed his golf clubs into the attic, and concentrated on baseball."[6]

The facts are slightly different.

I golfed several times at spring training on Catalina Island but rarely during the regular season.

Once I played a round with legendary pro golfer Sam Snead and Hank Sauer, a Chicago Cub teammate.

Another time I golfed after a game in Chicago. It was pitch dark when I hit a drive off the eighteenth tee. When I got to the ball on the fairway, I couldn't see the putting green; the caddy pointed it out for me. Amazingly, I hit the ball within four feet of the hole.

I've shot three holes in one, all after I retired from baseball. The third one was at the Athens Country Club and was worth $500 in products from the pro shop.

Golf great Sam Snead, center, used one of the sweetest swings in the history of the game to win eighty-two PGA tournaments. He's shown here with Ransom Jackson, left, and Hank Sauer, right, two of big-league baseball's best golfers. Ransom Jackson Collection.

What's amusing about this golf-and-baseball-don't-mix stuff is that most of the charity golf tournaments I competed in after leaving baseball featured ex-ballplayers. Maybe we were making up for the golfing we missed playing baseball.

One charity event in November 1952, sponsored by an Oklahoma oil tycoon, featured approximately thirty baseball players, including Mickey Mantle and Allie Reynolds of the New York Yankees. In addition to golf, we played baseball for three innings. At a party afterwards, the oil man asked if we'd be interested in hunting for polar bear in Alaska.

"I've got my own plane and all of the equipment needed," he said. "We could fly up to Alaska and return in about five days."

We got excited just thinking about a polar bear rug in front of our fireplaces.

"Do you know how to hunt polar bear?" he asked.

We had no idea, of course.

"You go out on a frozen lake, cut a hole in the ice about eight feet in diameter, open a can of peas, and spread them all around the hole," he explained. "When the polar bear comes up to take a pea, you kick him in the ice hole."

Mickey was standing next to me and laughed so hard, I thought he was going to fall down. By the way, we never got a chance to see if peas worked.

I wouldn't trade my experiences in baseball for anything but it was a job—a fun one but still a job. Golf was fun without the job part. I could do what I did as a kid at the Little Rock Country Club or at the home-made putt-putt course on the empty lot next door to our house. It was how I bonded with Dad and then later, friends, business colleagues, and my father-in-law, Percy "Skip" Yeargan.

Skip and I once played at the Willow Point Golf Course on Lake Martin near Alexander City, Alabama. The green for the eleventh hole is on a small island. The water level of the lake was lowered for the winter so we could see hundreds of golf balls in the sand. We picked up the balls like kids at an Easter egg hunt. We took a bunch of them to the beach in front of Skip's cabin on the lake and hit them across the water toward an island five hundred yards away.

Golf is as much about the journey as it is the destination. We were driving to a course in north Alabama, and nearly every town we passed through Skip had a story to tell from his days refereeing high school basketball and football games. The stories were as entertaining as the game itself.

I've played on some of the world's most beautiful golf courses, including the Augusta National Golf Club, home of the Masters, where I shot eighty for the par seventy-two course.

At the Colonial Country Club in Fort Worth, Texas, home course of golf great Ben Hogan, I was on the back nine with my partner, Frank Ruge, when out of nowhere appeared a fire truck–like golf cart with four members of the club and two caddies hanging on to the back. We bowed and let them play through.

The golf course I talk about the most is the one I just missed playing.

I was in Washington, D.C., for a baseball card show sponsored by Cub fans in the area when John Sununu, the former governor of New

Hampshire and chief of staff for President George H.W. Bush, invited a group of us to play at the exclusive and historic Congressional Country Club in Bethesda, Maryland. It was raining hard when we got there. All we could do was drown our sorrows at a bar near the eighteenth green. I really wanted to play that course.

When you think about it, golf brings out the kid in adults. It's an escape, a break from the daily routine that can make us feel robotic. It's a chance to enjoy the camaraderie of friends; swap golf tales, true and untrue; and quench your thirst on a hot summer day with a cold, frosty beer.

One of my favorite golf stories is from the Country Club of North Carolina in Pinehurst. There were twelve of us—six each from Georgia and North Carolina. We stayed in two big homes, grilled steaks outdoors, and stayed up all night playing poker. We played nine holes one day, thirty-six holes the next, and then eighteen holes. We started every morning with a buffet breakfast so large we could hardly swing the club on the first tee. The second hole was a par three peninsula hole. There were water hazards on three sides and a big pond on the right. One guy hit his tee shot plus four more balls into the water to end up with a ten for the hole. Watching all this from the balcony of a home at the end of the pond was a kindly gentleman who left his house and walked about one hundred feet to greet our waterlogged buddy at the next tee. He had a pitcher in his hand.

"Would you like a martini?" he asked.

"Hell, yeah!"

It was only 8:30 in the morning, but it was just what he needed.

A good friend and golf partner was Harold "Hokey" Jackson, one of Georgia's greatest high school football coaches. Things weren't going well for Hokie the second day of one tournament. As we came to the back nine, he excused himself for a few minutes. When he returned, there was a twinkle in his eye.

"Where did you go?" I inquired.

"I went to see Captain Jack."

That was Hokie's favorite bourbon. He kept a bottle in his clubhouse locker for situations like this. We won the tournament by two strokes.

I was golfing with another friend at the Athens Country Club. As he walked across a short causeway over a lake, he spotted a big bass splashing around in the water. He immediately took his shoes and socks off, rolled up his pants, jumped into the water, and started pounding the fish with a seven-iron. Suddenly, a man ran toward him, screaming, "Stop, that's my fish!" He had caught the bass and tied it to the shore to take home for dinner later. We weren't invited to join him.

Once I showed up for a tournament at the University of Georgia golf course to discover my partners were three guys who would never see eighty-five again. I was fifty-three at the time.

I quickly realized none of the trio could hit a drive more than 150 yards. I would hit the drive and the other guys would hit the ball onto the green with a short iron and then finish off the hole with a putter. They were masters with the short iron and putter, and we surprised everybody, including ourselves, by winning the tournament. I would've taken a selfie with the three smiling gentlemen but the iPhone had yet to be invented.

Prior to playing a golf course in southern Georgia, I was told to be on the lookout for wandering alligators. On one hole I hit a drive over a little rise and walked over to find my ball about twenty feet from an alligator, submerged in a nearby lake and looking right at me with his beady eyes.

"Move the ball and it's a two-stroke penalty," one of my golf mates quipped.

Whatever the sport, you're taught to keep both eyes on the ball. In this case, I kept one eye on the ball and the other on the twelve-foot alligator.

A regular at tournaments in Georgia was Bobo "No-Hit" Holloman. He always showed up in a truck pulling a trailer carrying a golf cart with "Bobo" written on the front of it. His son, Gary, caddied for him.

Bobo was just as brash and competitive on the fairway as he was on the pitcher's mound. "Often I would see a club in his golf bag broken in half," Bobo's wife, Nan, writes in her book, *This One and That One*. "I didn't suspect that he had thrown them against a tree when he had missed a shot."[7]

The only time I thought about throwing a golf club was when the alligator was eyeing me for lunch.

In one tournament I played in, a guy with a trumpet stood behind people teeing off at one of the holes situated near the water. If he blew the horn on your backswing, you were likely to blow the shot, topping the ball into the water.

I participated in a so-called cheater's tournament. You could cheat as much as you wanted but if you were caught, there was a two-stroke penalty. Everybody was watching everybody else. On the fifth hole, one of the guys checked the scorecard to see how everybody was doing. He discovered that the scorekeeper had recorded zeros for himself on the first four holes. Of course, he was cheating keeping score. Nobody thought about this, and he won the tournament.

At a two-day celebrity golf tournament hosted by singer-actor Pat Boone in Chattanooga, Tennessee, I sank every putt I walked up to and my team tied for first place. There were not enough trophies to go around, so Pat handed each member of my team a big golf umbrella. That was fine with us. Umbrellas work better in the rain.

I played football three years in college and baseball fifteen years as a collegian and pro. I played golf before football and baseball and long after I quit playing both. I never lost the love I had for golf as a kid. It's a four-letter word that I'll always spell L-O-V-E.

34

PILGRIMAGE TO WRIGLEY FIELD

Wrigley Field in Chicago marked its hundredth anniversary in 2014. All of the other major league ballparks I called home are gone or no longer used for baseball. So returning to Wrigley Field in 2011 at the age of eighty-five with my family was as special as the moments of glory I had playing there.

I'll always remember my first major-league homer in 1950, a game-winning shot in the tenth inning to beat the Brooklyn Dodgers; the chocolate donut and home run binge I went on in 1951; the tape-measure shot that ricocheted off the third floor of a Waveland Avenue apartment building in 1954; the tension and excitement of playing third base in Sam Jones's less-than-perfect but highly dramatic no-hitter in 1955.

I had been back to Wrigley Field only once since I played my final game September 25, 1959.

My visit in 2011 was the subject of a story in *Vineline*, the newsletter published by the Chicago Cubs.

"Before the *American Idol* judge, a Randy Jackson manned third base in Chicago," the article began. "An Arkansas native known as 'Handsome Ransom,' Jackson was around when Ernie Banks and Gene Baker integrated the Cubs in 1953."[1]

The Cubs were the eighth major-league team to sign blacks, the fourth in the National League. The Dodgers, of course, broke the color barrier with Jackie Robinson six years earlier. I wish the Cubs had more black players like Banks and Baker sooner. They became All-Stars in 1955 and the best double-play combination in the league.

The Cubs had three blacks in the starting lineup when I returned in 1959—Banks, second baseman Tony Taylor, and outfielder George Altman. Three more played occasionally—third baseman Don Eaddy and outfielders Lou Jackson and Billy Williams.

Taylor, a Cuban, went on to play nineteen years in the majors. Altman slugged 101 home runs in nine big-league seasons and 205 more in Japan where he played eight years. Williams batted .290 with 426 homers in a Hall of Fame career that spanned eighteen years.

Looking back on the integration of the Cubs, it was too little, too late.

The idea for the trip came from my son-in-law, Clay Bolton. The previous summer he called from Columbia, South Carolina, to say he wanted to take me and his son, Fowler, to Chicago for a game. Fowler had never been to Wrigley Field, and he wanted him to see a game with me in a ballpark where I once played.

Nothing happened, so in 2011 my oldest boys, Randy and Chuck, got involved and arranged an all-expense-paid trip for me and my wife, Terry, to fly to Chicago, stay in a downtown hotel, and attend a game between the Cubs and Dodgers, the teams I played with for most of my ten years in the majors.

When you hit the mid-eighty mark, you think twice before doing a lot of things, including buying green bananas. I figured this was going to be my last visit to Wrigley Field and said as much.

The trip soon became a family pilgrimage. Kids, grandkids, great-grandkids, in-laws, and their kin from South Carolina, Georgia, Mississippi, and Ohio, eagerly jumping on the bandwagon headed for Wrigleyville.

Two weeks before the game, I got a telephone call.

"Randy, how are you doing?" the man said. "I understand you're coming to Wrigley Field."

"I'm fine and, yes, I'm coming to Wrigley Field with my family," I replied. "Who is this?"

"Ernie Banks. I'll be in Chicago to see you."

We talked and talked about playing side by side at third base and shortstop for three full seasons and part of a fourth.

Ernie was called "Mr. Sunshine" as well as "Mr. Cub." He could even make you smile while you're eating a grapefruit. I was almost fired up the way my first Cub manager, Frank Frisch, thought I should be.

The memories were flowing.

There was the time Frank briefed a new Cub pitcher on what to throw Ralph Kiner, a great home run hitter for the Pittsburgh Pirates.

"Do not throw him a fastball," Frank said firmly. "Make it all curve-balls."

The pitcher threw Kiner a fastball, and he hit a towering fly ball that barely cleared a screen in front of the left-field wall. In most ballparks, it would've been caught for an out.

"Don't you remember what I told you about not throwing him a fastball?" Frank hollered when the pitcher got back to the dugout.

The next time Kiner batted, the pitcher followed Frank's instructions and tossed a curveball. He hit another homer, but there was nothing cheap about this one. It carried about 450 feet, high over the screen and well into the trees behind the wall.

When the inning was over, the pitcher walked straight up to Frisch in the dugout and said, "See there, Frankie, he hit your pitch farther than he did mine."

The guy was gone the next day.

Winning fifteen games for the Cubs in the fifties was no small accomplishment. In 1952, Warren Hacker, a farm boy from southern Illinois, pitched five shutouts in compiling a 15–9 record and 2.58 earned run average.

We were talking about hunting one day when Warren asked, "You know how I hunt rabbits? I hunt them with a slingshot and metal ball."

I thought he was pulling my leg until a teammate confirmed Warren could shoot down a running rabbit or squirrel from thirty yards away. He saw him do it.

Charlie Root, a Cub coach from 1951 to 1953, was the pitcher in the 1932 World Series when Babe Ruth supposedly pointed to the center-field bleachers at Wrigley Field and then hit a home run into the same area.

Charlie said he went along with the "called shot" because he didn't want to spoil a great tale. A better story, Charlie insisted, was a line drive caught by the center fielder after Babe sent the ball whistling between the pitcher's legs. The ball was about to be returned to the pitcher when he fainted from thinking about what might've been if the ball hadn't made it through his legs.

Walker Cooper, a backup catcher for the Cubs in 1954–55, was an easygoing guy but tough as a Mack truck. He played in 1,473 games over eighteen big-league seasons.

I'll always remember him walking into the clubhouse after one game with a big strawberry-red splotch on his butt from sliding on the hard ground. Most players would get the trainer to apply some salve and bandage up the wound. Not Walker. He picked up a bottle of rubbing alcohol, poured it on his hands, and then splashed it on the skin scraped raw. Several of us got nauseous watching him do it.

Today, there are all kinds of pads and protective gear for players to wear. To minimize arm injuries, teams strictly enforce pitch counts. Baseball is a kinder, gentler game.

There's also interleague play, the designated hitter, and video replays but, fundamentally, the game itself hasn't changed that much.

The business of baseball is altogether different.

In twelve years of pro baseball, I never met an agent and only had two paid endorsements—$250 for a children's glove that I have at home, and $100 for Lucky Strike cigarettes, which every Brooklyn Dodger received. I took the money but never tried the product because I don't smoke.

The teams I played for gave us uniforms, socks, hats, and a jacket. I had to pay for gloves, shoes, undershirts, shorts, jockstraps, and athletic protective cups.

My Kangaroo branded shoes cost $150 a pair. I wore a size 11 regular shoe and an 8½ baseball shoe. I soaked them in water and wore them during practice for three weeks so they would stretch and then tighten for a snug fit. To give my glove a big pocket, I wet it down, put a ball in it, and tied a string tightly around it.

All of these things were swirling through my mind on game day as we headed to Wrigley Field in a limousine.

Outside the main entrance, we mingled with fans, autographed copies of *Vineline*, and snapped pictures of each other standing next to the Ernie Banks statue and the iconic Wrigley Field marquee.

Inside, we went on a tour and posed for photos in front of the scoreboard reading "Randy 'Handsome Ransom' Jackson, former Chi-

Ransom Jackson and his grandson, Fowler Bolton, teamed to throw out the ceremonial first pitch prior to a Dodger-Cub game at Wrigley Field in 2011. The Cubs won the game, too. Ransom Jackson Collection.

cago Cub." Several of us were ushered into a room to meet Ernie and talk about the good old days for a documentary film he was doing.

The game was about to start.

I was scheduled to throw out the ceremonial first pitch. But I had a better idea I cooked up with the Cubs.

As I stepped onto the field with several members of my family, one ball was handed to me and another to my twelve-year-old grandson, Fowler. He looked at me and I said, "Come on."

Fowler followed me to the pitcher's mound, stopping a few feet in front of it. I motioned for Fowler to throw the ball to the waiting Cub catcher. He threw the first pitch, I tossed the second. The Cubs beat the Dodgers.

When Fowler got back home to Columbia, he was interviewed by television and radio stations. He was a local hero.

Of all the thrills I enjoyed at Wrigley Field, seeing my grandson throwing the first pitch that day was the greatest. It is the exclamation point at the end of Harry Caray's famous yell, "Holy cow!" It is the perfect ending for an ex-Cub called "Handsome Ransom."

Part 4

Ransom Thoughts

35

ONE FOR THE BOOK

The photograph was featured in the Sunday sports section of the *New York Times* July 15, 1951, but it was just as appropriate for the book section. The picture showed Chicago Cub manager Frank Frisch reading a book in the dugout during a game at Ebbets Field in Brooklyn. I'm sitting next to Frank with a big grin on my face.

In my twelve-year professional baseball career, I played in 1,356 games and never got ejected from any of them.

Umpire Dusty Boggess once called me out on strikes, and the next time I came to bat, he apologized: "Randy, I called you out on a bad pitch."

"Geez, why did you tell me?" I thought to myself.

Frisch never met an umpire that he liked. The same could be said for his players. In fact, he treated them alike.

One writer characterized his managerial style as "handicapped by a hot temper, impatience with youngsters, unfailing antagonism to umpires and his refusal to look at the calendar. He berated players on the bench, castigated them in the clubhouse."[1]

Frisch patterned himself after the first manager he played for in the 1920s, the tyrannical John McGraw, who was nicknamed "Little Napoleon."

Frank once sat on the bench twiddling his thumbs while Cub pitcher Walt "Monk" Dubiel burned on the mound in Philadelphia, walking six batters in the same inning, five of them in a row, to blow a four-run lead. He never bothered to have a relief pitcher warm up, explaining

Ransom Jackson was grinning as Cub manager Frank Frisch, sitting on his right, was reading a book in the dugout at Brooklyn's Ebbets Field. Frisch proceeded to throw the book onto the field in protest of an umpire's ruling. He was ejected for the third straight game. Ernie Sisto/The *New York Times*/Redux.

that he would have kept Dubiel in the game "for ninety-nine runs before he'd taken him out on that kind of performance."[2]

Even Phillies fans, not known for their brotherly love, felt sorry for Dubiel, shouting their disapproval over his public humiliation.

"I'm sick of watching some of my pitchers getting into jams, then peep out to the bullpen to see if a reliever is ready to take over his work for him," Frankie ranted afterwards.[3]

In one exhibition game, Frisch was coaching third base when I advanced from first to third on a play.

"You ran like a turtle," he cracked.

I was running from first to third again a couple of innings later on a single to right field. Recalling what Frisch said, I ran as fast as I could.

When he walked over to me, I said: "That was the fastest damn turtle you ever saw, wasn't it?"

He laughed and patted me on the back.

To cope with the fools he had to suffer, Frisch was "the readingest man in the majors."[4]

This quote from a *Chicago Tribune* article in 1950 says it all: "He has found serenity in his reading, specializing in books that teach relaxation thru such devices as counting up to ten before saying anything while sizzling, going barefoot whenever possible and not screaming at umpires, bartenders, photographers, sports writers, wild pitchers, fumbling infielders, hitless outfielders and other irritating characters."[5]

Frank was so calm after one day of reading and relaxation at his country estate in New Rochelle, New York, that he turned in two different batting lineups for a game in Brooklyn. The screw-up had Cub players batting out of order. His face "became redder than the blazing suns of thousands of baseball battlefields have ever made it," Edward Burns reported in the *Chicago Tribune*.[6]

I seemed to hit better when Frisch wasn't around. Against the Dodgers in Brooklyn, he was banished by three different umpires from three consecutive games. I homered twice in one game and had three hits, driving in five runs, in another.

Frank's streak in Brooklyn started after Pee Wee Reese stole home in the fourth inning of the series opener. He claimed Pee Wee was out and made his case by charging out of the dugout and going into one of his tirades.

The next day he was booted at the end of the first inning for arguing over ball-and-strike calls by the home plate umpire. As he left the dugout, he clasped a hand to his throat to let the ump know he choked up.

The third heave-ho came in the first game of a doubleheader when he tossed the book onto the field, shouting: "Here, read this while you're not doing anything."[7]

Frank was upset over the amount of time the Dodgers were allowed to replace starting pitcher Carl Erskine in the bottom of the fourth inning. Thinking it was a rule book, the home plate umpire tossed him out of the game.

Actually, Frank hurled a novel about Israel titled *Quiet Street*, a gift from Red Barber, the Dodgers' play-by-play announcer.

I always suspected Frisch went berserk in Brooklyn so he could leave early for his home in nearby New Rochelle and read one of the many books he had on flowers.

If Grant Dunlap had written his novel, *Kill the Umpire*, when we played together at Oklahoma City in 1949, I would've slipped Frank a copy to throw on the field. It was perfect for the occasion.

The central character in Dunlap's book, Ransome Burton, is haunted by an umpire, Dutch, who Ransome believes is out to get him. Dutch is behind the plate when Ransome comes up to bat in a crucial situation in the last game of the season. Ransome looks at what he's sure is ball four and a walk to load the bases. Instead, Dutch calls Ransome out on strikes. Suddenly, Ransome pulls a gun out of his back pocket and points it at Dutch.

Dunlap writes:

"A shot rang out. Dutch clutched his chest and crumbled to the ground.

"As bedlam and movement began, Ransome held up the gun and in a loud voice said, 'Everyone stay put.'

"To Dutch, he said, 'Stand up. That was just a blank. You aren't worth a real bullet.'

"To prove his point, Ransome fired the gun at his left arm. It was loaded with blanks." [8]

Of course, this is fiction. There was no Ransome Burton, no Dutch, no shooting. But when I think about Frisch throwing that book onto the field, I wish it had been *Kill the Umpire*. Lord knows, Frank wanted to.

36

THE MAN FROM MARS

It was around four o'clock in the afternoon. There wasn't anything to do where we were staying at the Schenley Hotel in Pittsburgh, Pennsylvania, so I walked to nearby Forbes Field with several other Chicago Cub players. We sat by ourselves in the grandstands, killing time before our game that night against the Pittsburgh Pirates.

The Pirates were taking batting practice. Up to the plate stepped a tall, gangly kid with long arms and big hands. He belted a pitch over the left-field wall and then, batting left-handed, dropped a shot into the right-field seats. He walked to the pitcher's mound and started throwing bullets. It was like watching Robert Redford play the imaginary Roy Hobbs in the movie *The Natural*. But this was really happening and we couldn't believe our eyes.

"Where in the world did they find this guy?" I asked.

"His fastball is one of the best I've ever seen," marveled Howie Pollet, a veteran Cub pitcher.

"He must've come directly from Mars," I said.

Phenoms come and go in baseball.

In early June 1955 when we saw "The Man from Mars" working out with the Pirates, they were commonly called bonus babies because most of them were fuzzy-cheeked kids signed right out of high school or college for large sums of money. A few like Al Kaline, Harmon Killebrew, and Sandy Koufax made it to the Hall of Fame. Most were busts and out of baseball soon after they got a dose of the big leagues.

The bonus baby era began in 1947, the year I signed with the Cubs. There was no cap on the bonuses teams could pay or how many they could sign. But they had to keep a bonus player on their active roster for a year. I signed a standard contract with the Cubs because I needed (and wanted) the experience of playing every day in the minors before facing major-league pitching. From 1953 through 1957, teams had to keep bonus players two full years after the signing date.

Bobby Bragan had three bonus pitchers on the 1956 Pirate team he managed and wasn't happy about it. "All they're doing is beating some-one out of a job who could help me on this club," he complained, noting: "I'll not use them unless I absolutely have to or one of them comes along awfully fast."[1]

One of the pitchers Bragan referred to was "The Man from Mars"— Paul "Big Jake" Martin, a six-foot-six, 235-pounder from Fayette City, Pennsylvania, a small town thirty miles south of Pittsburgh. He also was nicknamed "Jake the Preacher" because he was a minister in addition to being a local baseball legend.

He hit a five-hundred-foot home run when he was only fourteen. In Junior American Legion ball, he struck out twenty-three batters in a seven-inning game, only to lose 9–1 because the catcher couldn't hold on to his fastball. As a semipro, he pitched two no-hitters. "A blind man could see that guy has possibilities," said Ron Necciai, a Pirate pitching sensation himself three years earlier.[2]

Necciai lived in Monongahela, Pennsylvania, about six miles away from Charleroi, where the twenty-three-year-old Martin was a pitcher for the Charleroi Merchants, a semipro team. He took Martin to Pittsburgh for the tryout we witnessed. Three weeks later the Pirates signed him to a bonus contract. The scuttlebutt around the National League was he got $75,000. "My God," we thought, "that's a lot of money."

Martin actually got $30,000 payable in three annual installments. It was twice as much as I was making at the time.

Within hours of signing, Martin allowed two bloop hits in pitching three scoreless innings against the Boston Red Sox in an exhibition game. The *Charleroi Mail* reported that Martin "got off to a glowing start in what many believe will be a colorful pitching career in the big show."[3]

In his major-league debut against the Brooklyn Dodgers five days later, Martin pitched two more scoreless innings, striking out Jackie Robinson twice.

The Pirates had found the next superstar. It wouldn't be long before we'd see Big Jake in Chicago.

The Cubs were the first test for Ron Necciai when he broke into the majors with the Pirates in August 1952. Earlier that season pitching for Bristol, Tennessee, in the Class D Appalachian League, he struck out twenty-seven batters in a nine-inning game. That's something nobody ever did in professional baseball before or since. "Best pitching prospect I ever saw," catcher Joe Garagiola said of Necciai.

Garagiola was behind the plate when we jumped on Necciai for five runs in the first inning. He lost the game and finished the season and his big-league career with a 1–6 won-loss record and 7.08 earned run average. He hurt his pitching arm the following year and was out of baseball by the time Big Jake signed with the Pirates.

We didn't have 24/7 news coverage or sports talk shows to provide details of the five games Big Jake pitched before the Pirates rolled into Wrigley Field August 1. Word was spreading from team to team that he was deeply religious and afraid to throw as hard as he could because he might hurt somebody.

In his second game against the New York Giants, he started and threw only sixteen pitches. He walked three batters and hit another. In his next outing against the Philadelphia Phillies, he walked four of the five batters he faced. In five appearances totaling three and one-third innings, he walked twelve, almost four per inning.

Pirate general manager Branch Rickey wasn't discouraged.

"In fact the Fox of Forbes Field [Rickey] claims Martin can throw harder than any pitcher in the National League and possibly the American League and he has his hirelings working overtime on the Big Guy's control," *Charleroi Mail* sports editor Johnny Bunardzya wrote. He added: "Adjustments are in order and if all goes well, Big Jake will develop into the pitcher everybody expects him to be."[4]

The only scouting report the Cub hitters had was the one Pollet and I gave based on what we saw Big Jake do in his tryout. At one point, he knocked the glove off the catcher's hand with his fastball.

"You've got to be ready for this guy," I said in a clubhouse meeting at the start of a five-game series against the Pirates. "He throws BBs."

"I can't say much about his curveball but he throws hard," Pollet agreed.

"He can throw the ball so hard you almost can't see it," I added for emphasis.

Everybody was now curious about Big Jake. He finally appeared in the seventh inning of the second game, the Pirates trailing 11–4.

The first batter flied out, and then Gene Baker doubled, stole third base, and scored on a single. "Man, I'd like to hit against that guy all day long," Gene said back in the dugout. "That was like batting practice."

"Is this the same guy that we saw working out in Pittsburgh?" I asked Pollet.

"What do you mean, ready?" somebody else chided. "Anybody can hit that guy."

I took that personally because I grounded out.

Big Jake pitched two innings, giving up three hits and a run. He looked more like a preacher than a pitcher. His fastball needed prayer.

I lost track of Big Jake after the game in Chicago, even forgetting his name. Only recently did I find out what happened to him.

He pitched one more game in the majors, the Phillies racking up four hits and five earned runs against him in two innings. He walked four. He ended the season with seventeen walks and one hit batsman in seven and one-third innings pitched. He allowed thirteen hits and twelve runs, all earned. His earned run average was a whopping 15.21.

One story that made the rounds was that Big Jake went back home to count his money after he was released by the Pirates.

That's not entirely true.

He hurt the shoulder of his right throwing arm playing winter ball in the Dominican Republic. It was bothering him at spring training in 1956 when Bragan threw up his hands in frustration. "I can't figure out the boy," Bragan said. "His arm seems to hurt in a different spot each day. I'm through with him. I'm turning him over to Branch Rickey."[5]

Bunardzya explained the situation in his *Charleroi Mail* column: "It's no secret he just didn't take to the game like most red-blooded American kids do; most of them would give their eyeteeth for the chance to be a batboy let alone play for a big league team."[6]

A few days later the Pirates placed Martin on the voluntarily retired list. He waived the last two years of his bonus ($20,000) plus his annual salary of $6,000.

According to Bunardzya, Martin "signed a piece of paper which, in effect, said (1) He had a sore arm; (2) He didn't want to play professional baseball, and (3) He was willing to forget the whole thing if the Pirates wanted it that way."[7]

The way Big Jake crushed the ball in his tryout I always wondered why the Pirates didn't make an outfielder out of him. Obviously he had a higher calling.

"I felt baseball could bring me to the attention of more people and thus aid me in my ministerial ambitions," Martin said.[8]

Before joining the Pirates, Martin usually preached to a handful of people in an old, worn-out suit he called his "preacher suit." Afterwards, he had three new suits and was speaking to crowds numbering in the hundreds.

He was a minister for several more years and then became a chiropractor. He established a practice in San Diego, California, where he lived until his death in 2011.

Big Jake had everything in the world one afternoon in Pittsburgh. The *Sporting News* summed it up best: "The tricks he did with a baseball—either pitching or batting—made everybody's eyes pop."[9]

I'll always remember Big Jake as "The Man from Mars."

37

MY ROOMIES

Roommates are a thing of the past in Major League Baseball. That's too bad because some of baseball's best stories were inspired by players rooming together during spring training or on road trips.

The mother of all roommate tales is the 1914 Ring Lardner classic, *My Roomy*, about Buster Elliott, a player who scared off roommates with his eccentric behavior. Buster insisted on having the water run in the bathtub all night to remind him of the sound of the dam near his home. Another quirk was turning on the lights in the middle of the night so he could lather up and shave with a straight razor in front of the dresser mirror.

The worst part, according to one roommate, was "he'd stop shavin' every little while and turn round and stare at the guy who was makin' a failure o' tryin' to sleep. Then he'd wave his razor round in the air and laugh, and begin shavin' agin. You can imagine how com'table his roomies felt!"[1]

Buster was fictional; Babe Ruth was real. Babe's roommates weren't too sure because he was never in the hotel room assigned to him. "I don't room with Ruth," said Ping Bodie, one of his New York Yankee roommates. "I room with his suitcase."[2]

Two of my teammates with the Chicago Cubs were Steve Bilko, a beer-loving first baseman, and Jim Brosnan, a pitcher who went on to become a best-selling author. They roomed together in the minors, providing stories that Brosnan wrote about later.

"The best thing he could do was the thing that he did—drink beer," Brosnan said of Bilko. "He would buy beer incidentally. There are a lot of beer drinkers who don't buy beer. But he'd buy them in order to keep people around drinking with him. I think that's a good attribute. I had a few beers on ol' Steve. When he ordered those six-packs up in the hotel, he ordered one for me."

A good roommate was a guy you shared a beer and a laugh with after a game.

One of my roommates with the Brooklyn Dodgers was Dick Williams, a versatile infielder-outfielder. After a Sunday afternoon game against the Cardinals in St. Louis, we stopped at a bar to have a couple of beers before boarding the team bus for our next stop.

The bar was crowded and noisy. We had to yell to hear each other across the table.

"Dick," I said, "let me tell you a story about Chuck Connors at spring training."

Chuck was with me and two other Cub players at a restaurant in Avalon on Catalina Island.

"I'm going to do something," Chuck said. "Don't any of you look up."

As we looked down at the table, Chuck hollered a cuss word as loud as he could. When we looked up and around at the other people in the restaurant, there was no reaction.

We had a couple of beers.

"Let's try it here!" Dick said.

"Okay," I said, "you go first."

Dick picked a word that would've got him thrown out of a game. Nobody looked at us.

"My turn."

I yelled another swear word. We did this five times, trying different words and laughing after each one. Not a soul in the bar paid any attention to us.

"Doesn't that prove that the Chuck Connors story is true?"

"Yeah," Dick said, "that was fun."

Dick played thirteen years in the majors and then managed twenty-one more, leading the Boston Red Sox to the American League pennant in 1967; the Oakland Athletics to World Series titles in 1972 and 1973; and the San Diego Padres to the National League championship in 1984. He was inducted into the Hall of Fame as a manager in 2008.

Roger Craig was another Dodger roommate who became a successful big-league manager, guiding the San Francisco Giants to two division titles as well as the National League pennant in 1989. He managed the Giants for eight years and the San Diego Padres for two. Prior to that he was a pitching coach for the Padres, Houston Astros, and Detroit Tigers, best known for teaching the split-finger fastball to Mike Scott, a twenty-game winner for the Astros in 1989, and Jack Morris, winner of 254 games in an eighteen-year career that spanned from 1977 to 1994.

Roger pitched twelve years in the majors, seven for the Dodgers and two nightmarish seasons for the New York Mets when he lost twenty-four and twenty-two games in successive seasons. He was in his first full season with the Dodgers when we roomed together in 1956.

We were Southern boys who had a lot in common from the movies we watched to the occasional beer and steak we enjoyed together. Roger was the perfect roommate and one of the few I've kept in contact with over the years.

Roger was managing the Giants when I took my wife, Terry, and son, Ransom Baxter, to Wrigley Field in the 1980s to see the Giants and Cubs play. Before the game, we talked about how baseball had changed since our playing days. The biggest difference, of course, is the multi-million-dollar contracts that are common today. Some of the players don't know what to do with their money or lives. "They are rich and have a lot of ability," Roger said, "but they need a lot of guidance." As we chatted, I realized that thirty-something years later we were still on the same page.

I've forgotten the name of my first Dodger roommate but not his politeness.

"Good morning, Mr. Jackson," he greeted me every day during spring training.

"I'm not Mr. Jackson," I kept saying, pointing out that I was thirty and not much older than him.

"Good morning, Mr. Jackson," he persisted.

"God almighty, I'm not Mr. Jackson."

Don Drysdale was a twenty-year-old pitching phenom who I should've called mister because he wound up in the Hall of Fame. I was his roommate when the Dodgers visited Japan in late 1956, but as far as

Ransom Jackson and pitcher Roger Craig, right, enjoy a few appetizers at a Dodger reception. They roomed together on the road during the 1956 season. Ransom Jackson Collection.

the Japanese girls were concerned, I was his chaperone. Tall, handsome, and single, he was a big hit with women fans.

When we went to breakfast in the morning, there was always a group of attractive girls waiting for him in the hotel lobby. He sat and talked with them in one corner while I twiddled my thumbs in another. If I had taken some knitting with me, I could've knitted a sweater. It was fun to watch—everywhere we went, a bevy of girls followed Don.

We hit it off so well in Japan that when the month-long tour ended, Don decided to come home with me to Athens, Georgia, and stay a few days.

The Dodgers' pairing of twenty-year-old Don Drysdale, right, with thirty-year-old Ransom Jackson as roommates on their goodwill tour of Japan in 1956 worked beautifully. When the month-long trip ended, Drysdale followed Jackson home to Athens, Georgia. Ransom Jackson Collection.

Long after we both retired from baseball, he called to ask for help in finding an apartment for his daughter, Kelly, who was going to study journalism at the University of Georgia in Athens. When they arrived in late December, we showed them around town and then took them to a New Year's Eve party at the Athens Country Club. Jaws dropped as people immediately recognized Don. He was the center of attention, just like in Japan.

The Christmas card list for most baseball players is short. The guy sitting at the locker next to you in the clubhouse could be traded, released, or sent down to the minors at any time. It was here today, gone tomorrow. The constant turnover made it tough to build lasting relationships.

One player who sent me a Christmas card every year was Bob Kelly, a pitcher and roommate for part of a season with the Cubs. We started our pro careers at Des Moines, and played together briefly in Los Angeles and Springfield before landing in Chicago.

There was an incident during spring training with the Cubs that I always associated with Bob, although he eventually set me straight in a letter, saying I had the wrong guy. Anyway, it's a good story and worth telling.

This pitcher, not to be confused with Bob, was throwing batting practice before an exhibition game at Wrigley Field in L.A. I was at third base when the pitcher got hit smack-dab between the legs by a one-hop smash up the middle. He wasn't wearing a protective cup. I rushed over to him as he was writhing in pain on the ground. I swear he was turning green.

"Shoot me!" he pleaded. "Shoot me!"

That's all he could say as they carried him off the field.

I was ready to shoot Bob Ramazzotti, an infielder and my roomie to begin the 1952 season with the Cubs. He was a good guy with a bad habit of smoking thin, curved Italian cigars. I'd open the door of our hotel room and the smoke from the cigars was so dense that I couldn't see the other side of the room. After a week, I asked to move. "I can't breathe in that room," I told Bob Lewis, the team's traveling secretary.

He paired me with Hal Jeffcoat, a weak-hitting, strong-armed outfielder the Cubs converted into a pitcher. We were rooming together in 1953 when the *Chicago Sun-Times* ran a series of articles titled "Baseball's Glamor Boys." I was compared with James Mason, a British movie actor, and Hal with James Cagney, a film star famous for playing tough-guy roles.

Outfielder Hank Sauer was likened to actor Cary Grant because of "his steel-like eyes and the lined, weather-beaten look on his face."[3]

Shortstop Roy Smalley was called "Mr. Snakehips" and considered a look-alike for actor Peter Lawford.[4]

Utility infielder Bill Serena's "upcurled eyelashes" were the envy of female fans, reporter Virginia Marmaduke wrote, noting: "They say that to be another Desi Arnaz, all he needs is Lucille Ball."[5]

According to the women interviewed, I had "soft, brown eyes, a chiseled face and the kind of 'little boy' stuff that adds up to swoon stuff. He is the top glamor boy to the lipstick set and they either want to 'mother' him or 'date' him—according to their ages."[6]

Eddie Gold and Art Ahrens had a different view in their book, *The New Era Cubs*, published in 1985. "Actually, he resembled a Gregory Peck with meat on his bones."[7]

To women fans, Hal was a younger, taller version of Cagney. "They have the same pugnacious personality and even look a little bit alike," Marmaduke quoted one admirer. "I sometimes say a prayer for Jeffcoat when he steps to the plate."[8]

Judging from the reaction of the ladies, we would've been better off doing movies in Hollywood than playing for the Cubs.

I don't recall ever getting a Christmas card from Hal, but one winter he sent me a box with three live lobsters. They scurried around the kitchen floor until we caught and cooked them. They were delicious—one more reason I liked rooming with Hal.

Another favorite was Yosh Kawano, the Cubs' longtime equipment manager.

Midway during the 1954 season my wife, Ruth, went home to Athens with our newborn son, Randy. I moved into an apartment near Wrigley Field with three other players and Yosh. We shared the same room.

No detail was too small for Yosh.

"He used to keep an envelope in his back pocket, and he could tell you what size shoe Alvin Dark wore, what size shirt Alvin Dark wore," Billy Williams said on Yosh's retirement in 2008.[9]

Many nights I was in bed half-asleep when Yosh got in from work. If the blankets weren't snugly around my neck, he pulled them up to keep me warm.

All the Cubs' home games were played during the day so two or three times a week we went to a small restaurant-bar near our apartment to eat and watch a young local comedian with big, sad eyes, a flattop haircut, and dry sense of humor. "I have a drink or two on occasion—like when the sun goes down," he deadpanned. "I have never been known to touch a drop during a total eclipse."

He talked about being a fighter pilot in Oklahoma during World War II. "If you think back, there's not one Japanese aircraft that got past Tulsa."

The comedian did his act and then sat down at our table to visit. We became friends and I gave him free tickets to the games. Later on, I took Ruth to see him at a bigger venue in Chicago.

The comedian soon had his own television series and appeared frequently on *The Tonight Show* with Johnny Carson. When he joined Bob Hope and Dean Martin on one program, he asked Johnny: "Did you ever get the feeling that the world is a tuxedo and you're a pair of brown shoes?"[10]

In 1958 the comedian was performing at a dinner club in Los Angeles while I was playing for the Dodgers. I booked a table for four and took Ruth, Don Drysdale, and his date. After the show, Ruth and I were invited backstage by the now-famous comedian—George Gobel. Don and his friend were not included. It was the first and last time anyone wanted to see me rather than Don.

38

OF POWER PITCHERS AND POWDER PUFFS

There were no radar guns in the 1950s to measure the speed of a pitcher's fastball and display it instantaneously in the ballpark for crowds to ooh and ah about. It didn't matter because there were plenty of power pitchers to light up the fans and the hitters. But they weren't the pitchers who sent me home hitless and clueless as to what happened.

One of the toughest pitchers for me to hit was a guy named Casimir James "Jim" Konstanty, who wore glasses, looked like a college professor, and had a fastball like one, too. You could almost catch him barehanded.

Jim had a bachelor's degree in physical education from Syracuse University as well as assorted powder-puff pitches that he threw at some thirty different speeds ranging from forty miles per hour up to possibly eighty-five.

Konstanty was the National League's Most Valuable Player in 1950, posting a 16–7 record and 2.66 earned run average as a relief pitcher for the pennant-winning Philadelphia Phillies. He also had twenty-two saves, although nobody was keeping count at the time.

On seeing Konstanty warm up for the first time, most hitters smiled and confidently said, "Give me a bat."

Konstanty never tried throwing the ball past a hitter. He wanted you to hit it. And you usually did. First time up, you might fly out. Second time, you popped up or grounded out. At the end of the game, you were typically 0-for-4 and checking your bat for holes.

Jim struck me out only once, but all I had to show for my first fifteen at bats against him was a walk and two hits. Eventually, I stopped swinging hard and wound up with a .300 batting average (9-for-30) over a six-year period.

Another pitcher who gave me fits was knuckleballer Hoyt Wilhelm. For twenty-one seasons (1952–72), he baffled nearly everybody, including his catchers, to earn a spot in the Hall of Fame with 143 wins, 227 saves, and a 2.51 earned run average, the lowest of any pitcher with two thousand–plus innings after 1927.

The unpredictable pitch was the subject of the 2012 documentary *Knuckleball!* that focused on the careers of two recent practitioners, Tim Wakefield of the Boston Red Sox and R.A. Dickey when he was with the New York Mets.

"Once it leaves your hand it's up to the world what it's going to do," Dickey said in the film.[1]

"Everything you're taught as a catcher goes out the window," said Jason Varitek, one of Wakefield's catchers during a nineteen-year career that saw him win two hundred games.[2]

"I don't think he knows where it's going," New York Yankee shortstop Derek Jeter said of Wakefield's knuckleball.[3]

Mike Hargrove, a solid .290 hitter over twelve seasons in the majors, once was asked how to hit a knuckleball. "Stick your tongue out the left side of your mouth in the even innings," he said, "and out the right side in the odd innings."[4]

"It is erratic," said Charlie Hough, a knuckleballer who won 216 games in the majors. "When it is not done well, it's really bad."[5]

I had a front row seat at third base for two knuckleballers with the Chicago Cubs: Willie "The Knuck" Ramsdell and Emil "Dutch" Leonard.

Prior to joining the Cubs in 1952, Willie pitched for the Brooklyn Dodgers and Cincinnati Redlegs. He won only twenty-four games in the majors because, as Dodger manager Leo Durocher lamented, "every time he winds up, he practically advertises 'here comes my knuckler but I defy you to hit it.'"[6]

I batted .444 against Willie, getting four hits in nine at bats, so I liked it better when he was on the other side.

In a Kodak moment against Willie and the Cubs, Jackie Robinson stole home with a picture-perfect hook slide. "Goddamn," Willie shouted at catcher Johnny Pramesa. "You shoulda got him."[7]

"Hey, Will," Jackie yelled during batting practice the next day. "Why'd you hold the ball so long?"

Still agitated, Ramsdell hollered back: "So you could get your goddamn picture in the paper."[8]

Jackie didn't find Dutch very amusing.

"I'm glad of one thing," he said after his rookie season with the Dodgers in 1947, "and that is, I don't have to hit against Dutch Leonard every day. Man, what a knuckleball that fellow has. It comes up, makes a face at you, then runs away."[9]

They weren't smiley faces either because Dutch won 191 games in twenty big-league seasons.

Knuckleballers get better with age and seemingly last forever. Dutch was forty-four when he finally quit, Wakefield forty-five, Hough forty-six, Phil Niekro forty-eight, and Wilhelm forty-nine.

Dean Chance, a Cy Young Award winner for the Los Angeles Angels in 1964, and Wilhelm were teammates briefly for the Baltimore Orioles in 1960. "After the first day of spring training, I always stood beside him," Chance said. "He threw a knuckleball that damn near tore my nuts off."[10]

Three of the five hits I got off Wilhelm the thirty-seven times we faced each other came during his rookie season with the New York Giants. Strung together, the three hits barely reached third base. Overall, I batted .147 against Hoyt.

The knuckleball is a freak pitch that only a select few throw effectively. The curveball is in every pitcher's arsenal and public enemy number one for hitters. The biggest killer is the overhand curve because it breaks straight down and is equally devastating to right-handers and left-handers.

Warren Spahn, a Hall of Fame left-hander, won twenty games or more in thirteen seasons, the last time when he was forty-two years old. He had a high leg kick and threw directly overhand, causing the ball to rise on its approach to home plate. This made his fastball nastier, his curve and changeup fantastic. Lifetime, I batted .238 against Spahn. In one game, I grounded into three double plays, two of them on balls hit right back to him.

The pitcher who struck me out the most was another Hall of Famer, Robin Roberts (seventeen), followed by three Dodgers: Russ Meyer (thirteen), Don Newcombe (eleven), and Carl Erskine (ten).

Roberts threw hard with the same overhand motion and was always around the plate. I had more hits (twenty-four), triples (seven), and runs batted in off Robin than any other pitcher, but he still held me to a .231 batting average. By comparison, I batted .304 against Erskine and homered four times each against Meyer and Newcombe.

Erskine had a great curveball and changeup to go with a good fastball, and Newcombe was a pure power pitcher. To beat the Cubs, Meyer just showed up.

Russ broke in with the Cubs in 1946 and pitched at my tryout the following year. The Cubs traded him in late 1948, and over the next seven years, he tormented them by compiling a 24–3 record—the best ever against the Cubs. Our paths crossed again in the 1955 trade that sent me to the Dodgers and Russ back to the Cubs where he won just one more game.

Like most ballplayers, I'm proud of every hit. But one in particular stands out because it was against the most intimidating pitcher of my era—Ewell "The Whip" Blackwell of the Cincinnati Redlegs.

There were no batting helmets to protect you from the hundred-mile-per-hour fastballs that the six-foot-six Blackwell delivered with a whiplike sidearm motion. He led the National League in hit batsmen six times. "I was a mean pitcher," Blackwell admitted. [11]

Another hard thrower, Sandy Koufax, said, "Pitching is . . . the art of instilling fear." [12]

"Ewell Blackwell was a scary pitcher," said Ralph Kiner, a fearless home run slugger most of the time. "Your legs shook when you tried to dig in on him." [13]

In fourteen at bats against Blackwell, I walked three times and had just one hit. But, oh, what a hit it was. My legs stopped shaking long enough for me to crack a two-run homer off "The Whip."

39

THE CHEATING GAME

Baseball players in the 1950s didn't use performance-enhancing drugs, but that doesn't mean they weren't looking for ways to break the rules and get that competitive edge.

Ernie Johnson was a relief pitcher for the Braves in Boston and Milwaukee before the team moved to Atlanta, and he became the voice of the Braves as a color commentator and play-by-play announcer on television and radio.

Ernie relied on finesse instead of speed, so when he struck out the first two batters on fastballs one night in Milwaukee, they returned to the dugout muttering, "I've never seen Ernie throw that hard."

We watched his first pitch to the next batter closely and noticed he was standing about eight inches in front of the pitching rubber. A few inches can make a big difference. We complained that Ernie was cheating, the home plate umpire told him to stop, and his fastball returned to normal.

Corked bats were not uncommon. When discovered, an umpire threw out the bat but let the hitter remain in the game.

In many cases, someone associated with the teams did the dirty work.

At Philadelphia's Shibe Park, the groundskeeper fixed the infield to take advantage of the outstanding bunting ability and speed of the Phillies' biggest star, Richie Ashburn, a .308 hitter during his fifteen years in the majors. On seeing him as a rookie, one sportswriter reported, "He's no .300 hitter; he hits .100 and runs .200."[1]   •

Richie's specialty was a running bunt, dragging the ball down the first-base line as he sprinted out of the left side of the batter's box. The lime chalk marking the first- and third-base foul lines was raised just high enough to keep a slow-rolling ball fair instead of going foul. To slow down the ball, the infield grass was allowed to grow a little longer than usual. Richie averaged thirty to thirty-five bunt singles a year.

The infield at Sportsman's Park in St. Louis where the Cardinals and Browns played was like concrete. Balls took one bounce and rocketed over the heads of infielders. You needed life insurance to play third base. When Gerald Staley was pitching for the Cardinals, the grounds crew watered the area in front of home plate so batters would beat his sinker balls into the ground for easy outs.

Stealing a catcher's signs to the pitcher was the most widespread form of cheating.

Ray Blades, a third-base coach for the Cubs, was a master at it. He stood as close to the foul line as possible to get a good look at the catcher's signs. He had great eyes and if the catcher's legs were too far apart, he could see the number of fingers indicating the pitch to follow. He had a whistle for one finger and another for two. The whistle told the batter what was coming. If you didn't hear it and guessed wrong, you were on your own.

The hand-operated scoreboard at Chicago's Wrigley Field was ideal for stealing a catcher's signs.

Cub players were informed that one of the number slots would be left empty so a scoreboard operator could use his feet to communicate with the batter. If you saw one foot in the tiny hole, it was going to be a fastball. Two feet was a curveball.

My eyes weren't that good. I could see the scoreboard and the slot. But I had trouble seeing the shoes. I'd look and think I saw one shoe and it was two. Or vice versa. Needless to say, cheating didn't make me a better hitter.

One of the most intriguing characters I played against was Lew Burdette, winner of 203 games in eighteen big-league seasons. He threw overhand, sidearm, underhand, any way humanly possible. He also was widely suspected of doctoring the ball with Vaseline or some other substance. The home plate umpire often stopped the game to examine the first finger on his throwing hand for evidence of cheating.

"There isn't a pitching rule he doesn't break," said Birdie Tebbetts, manager of the Cincinnati Redlegs. "He spits on the ball, he spits on his glove, he spits on his hand, he rubs the ball on his uniform."[2]

Lew went through all kinds of contortions on the mound, touching his lips and cap while pulling up his pants by the belt. The ritual caused Fred Haney, his manager with the Milwaukee Braves, to remark, "Burdette would make coffee nervous."[3]

Birdie stopped short of accusing Lew of throwing an illegal spitball by saying, "If he's not throwing it, then he's missing a heck of a chance."[4]

Lew always played it cagey. "Why, I think Birdie was trying to get my goat. He majored in psychology, you know."[5]

I had only eleven hits to show for the forty-nine times I batted against Lew. If you're keeping score, that's a .224 batting average.

I saw pitches come up close to the plate and then drop suddenly at a forty-five-degree angle. Most batters thought Lew was concealing Vaseline at one of the touch points in his fidgeting routine. But nobody could figure it out, and he continued to dazzle us.

In Brooklyn one night he threw a pitch that plummeted between the catcher's legs. Our batboy recovered the ball and brought it back to the dugout for closer inspection. It was completely clean except for one dirt spot about one-eighth of an inch high and the size of a fingertip.

Thirty years after retiring I was with some golf buddies in Sea Island, Georgia. We were sitting in a hotel bar waiting to go to dinner and in walked Lew, looking to play a round of golf the next day. We invited him to join us.

As we played, we talked about old times. I was waiting for the right moment to ask Lew the big question. It came as we were walking down the fairway after teeing off on the eighteenth hole.

"Lew," I said, "it has been thirty years since we played and I swear by my Cub Scout honor that I won't say anything. But did you doctor the baseball?"

Lew stopped, looked at me, smiled, and kept on walking. He left me guessing. And that's the way it should be.

40

HEAVEN ON EARTH

The scene lasts only five seconds, but it's the most memorable one in *Field of Dreams*, the movie about Iowa farmer Ray Kinsella transforming part of his cornfield into a baseball park.

"Is this heaven?" Shoeless Joe Jackson asks as he runs onto the pristine outfield grass, tall stalks of corn serving as a natural fence.

"No, it's Iowa," Kinsella answers.

The Chicago Cub teams in the 1950s played like hell at times, but our home ballpark of Wrigley Field was always heaven. What made playing there even more heavenly was all games were during the day.

Most players see the ball better in the daylight. The difference for me was literally night and day. In 378 home games with the Cubs, I batted .277 as compared with .252 on the road. Counting two home runs I hit with the Dodgers, fifty-one of my 103 career homers came at Wrigley Field.

The disparity became greater as I got older. In 1953 at age twenty-seven, I hit .322 at Wrigley Field and .241 elsewhere. In 1955, my home-and-away numbers were .287 and .231. In 1959, my last season, they were .313 and .179.

My eyes were never tested, but it's doubtful I ever had twenty-twenty vision.

I never saw the spin on the ball that modern-day color commentators talk so much about. In fact, I had to squint to see the ball, especially when there were fans in the center-field bleachers at Wrigley Field.

Not even cold weather could dampen the enjoyment of playing day games at Wrigley Field for Ernie Banks, left, playing pepper with Ransom Jackson, center, and Gene Baker. Ransom Jackson Collection.

Today's ballparks have a green backdrop behind center field so hitters can see the ball better. We didn't have that luxury in the 1950s. Often we had to look for the ball coming out of a sea of white shirts.

The worst part about playing at Wrigley Field was Sunday doubleheaders when the center-field bleachers were full and as white as snow. It was hard to see.

I was able to overcome some of my vision problems because of excellent depth perception. Years later when I was taking flying lessons, my instructor said, "Your hands are too quick. Be gentle when you make a turn."

I was one of several players to participate in an experiment with amber-colored glasses that were supposed to make lights brighter. We tested the glasses before a night game at Sportsman's Park in St. Louis.

I wore them during batting and infield practice and to start the game. I could see the ball better, but the glasses were big and bulky. After two innings, nobody was wearing them. "Thank you so much," I said, "but you can take them back to where they came from."

Wrigley Field would still be without lights if Philip K. Wrigley were alive and owned the Cubs. "With everyone else gone night baseball crazy, we are now pioneering in day baseball at Wrigley Field," he quipped in 1953.[1]

The acquisition that year of slugger Ralph Kiner renewed attention to the issue of day baseball: "There is no question that day baseball adds several seasons to a player's career," Kiner said on joining the Cubs.[2]

This was music to Wrigley's ears.

"We have Social Security, pensions, Blue Cross—everything to make people live longer," he said. "We will have older people with more leisure time and money. Night baseball shuts out many of these people. It also shuts out our fans of tomorrow, the youngsters who can't come roaming home at midnight from ball games."[3]

Racetracks primarily operate during the day and attract more people than baseball, Wrigley reasoned. "Baseball is by nature a day game. The fans get more enjoyment out of it, then, and there is no question that the players like it much better than night ball."[4]

Wrigley remained steadfast, declaring nearly a decade later: "We don't need lights in Wrigley Field, we need a contender."[5]

Nobody could dispute that.

In 1981 the Tribune Company, a media conglomerate, purchased the Cubs from the Wrigley family. By the end of the 1988 season Wrigley Field had lights—"fifty-three years, two months and fifteen days after the debut of big-league baseball under the arcs."[6]

It was necessary financially, but I hated to see it. I wasn't alone.

"It's a mustache on the Mona Lisa, plastic flamingos fronting the Taj Mahal," columnist Ray Sons wrote. "Anyone who would celebrate this is a dim bulb with no appreciation of what has made Wrigley Field, and the Cubs, special."[7]

A standing-room-only crowd of forty thousand showed up for the first night game against the Philadelphia Phillies on August 8, 1988.

"You'd have thought an extraterrestrial being was going to land on the field," the Phillies' Mike Schmidt said. "The damned baseball game didn't have a whole lot of meaning. It was nothing but an excuse to party."[8]

Morganna Roberts, "The Kissing Bandit," scampered onto the field but was stopped by security guards before she could reach home plate and her target, Ryne Sandberg of the Cubs. "It was kind of fun, kind of loosened me up, and I ended up having a good at-bat," said Sandberg, who proceeded to hit a two-run homer.[9]

"I think it's great," said Mr. Cub, also known as Ernie Banks. "Let's play three."[10]

Ernie was overruled.

In the third inning there were flashes of lightning followed by thunder and monsoon-like rains in the fourth. The game was called off two hours and ten minutes later.

"It looked like the Good Lord said, 'I'm going to show you why Wrigley Field has always been in daylight,'" Cub pitcher Rick Sutcliffe said. "He was pretty upset about this. He's telling us he'll determine when the first night game is."[11]

The game was televised nationally, but I didn't watch. I turned the channel while Mr. Wrigley rolled over in his grave.

Sutcliffe best summed up my feelings when he said: "It was more sad than exciting. It was like two old friends saying goodbye to each other—sunshine and Wrigley Field."[12]

41

THE BAT THAT GLOWED

A favorite pastime of ex-ballplayers is telling stories about their careers. The stories often are embellished, the imagination filling in the blanks of a foggy memory.

I was one of many former major leaguers who participated in a charity golf tournament and dinner event held annually in Ringgold, Georgia. Hall of Famer Joe Sewell was the after-dinner speaker one year.

Joe played from 1920 to 1933, spending eleven seasons with the Cleveland Indians and three with the New York Yankees, where one of his teammates was Babe Ruth.

Joe talked about the time the Yankees were about to start a road game and Babe was missing. Joe went to the clubhouse and found him on a table with his pants on backwards, still tipsy from drinking the night before. The clubhouse boy helped a laughing Babe turn his pants around. Joe ushered him to the field and pointed him to the Yankee dugout. Babe sat down. He was still sitting in the top of the first inning when it was time to hit.

"Someone helped him up and put a bat in his hand," Joe said. "Babe hit the second pitch up in the seats. He wasn't even sure of the name of the town where the team was playing."

The story is one of those you had to be there to know if it was entirely true.

But there's no doubt Joe was the hardest guy to strike out in major-league history. You can look it up. He struck out only three times in two

The Brooklyn Dodgers infield, left to right, of third baseman Ransom Jackson, shortstop Pee Wee Reese, second baseman Don Zimmer, and first baseman Gil Hodges held their bats in the shape of a baseball diamond during a photo session at spring training in Vero Beach, Florida. Ransom Jackson Collection.

seasons and four times in three others. In 7,132 career at bats, he struck out 114 times. What's most amazing is Joe used the *same* bat.

After being inducted into the National Baseball Hall of Fame in 1977, he gave the bat to the Hall of Fame to display. When he checked on the bat several years later, he found out it was in a storage room where nobody could see it. He took it back home with him to Alabama.

When Joe died in 1990, his obituary in the *New York Times* didn't mention the Hall of Fame part of the bat story. It did report that Joe "used only one bat during his entire major league career . . . a 35-inch, 40-ounce Ty Cobb model Louisville Slugger he kept in condition by seasoning it with chewing tobacco and stroking it with a Coke bottle."[1]

I struck out a lot more than Sewell (382 times in 3,549 at bats). But I was just as protective of my bat, a Louisville Slugger K-55 that was thirty-five inches long and weighed thirty-two ounces. I also have my own bat story that I've told many times over the years.

When I first got to the majors, old-timers like Sewell said the secret to a great bat was a wide grain. If I could find one with a knot in the wood, that was the Holy Grail.

At spring training I opened a box of custom-made bats with my name on them. I examined them carefully. There was one particular bat that glowed with stars flying out of it. This was the bat I was looking for. The grains were wide and there was a knot in the middle of the sweet spot.

I didn't use the bat in spring training, saving it for the games that really counted. I checked on the bat regularly, even joking that I slept with it at night.

The Cubs opened the season in St. Louis at Sportsman's Park. On the mound for the Cardinals was Gerald Staley, a pitcher with a sinker ball that hitters typically pounded into the ground for easy outs.

The bases were loaded when I walked to the plate in the first inning holding the greatest bat in the world. I swung at the first pitch. Krraaack!!!

The bat cracked in my hand, the ball flying weakly over the shortstop for a bloop single, driving in two runs. What a glorious death!

That's the story I've always told and believed to be true until someone tried to verify it. According to the box score, I didn't start the game. When I pinch-hit in the ninth inning, the bases weren't full. And, worst of all, my single didn't score two runs.

Box scores don't lie, and they don't distinguish a bloop single from a line drive. My version of the story is better, and it's how I choose to remember the bat that glowed. Its life was short and a perfect 1-for-1, worthy of a place in a storage room at the Hall of Fame.

42

A FISHING TALE THAT'S MOSTLY TRUE

There are some fishing stories too good to believe. This is one of them.

Many years after I retired from baseball, we had a yard sale at our home in Athens, Georgia. One of the items offered was a tarpon I caught fishing in Biscayne Bay near Miami with several of my new Brooklyn Dodger teammates during spring training of 1956.

Piloting the boat was Roy "Campy" Campanella, the greatest catcher I ever saw and one of the nicest and best teammates. He appreciated where he was and how he got there. He never met anybody he didn't like. He lifted the spirits of everybody around him.

Campy loved being around the water and sharing that love with others. On this fishing expedition, there was me; pitchers Carl Erskine, Roger Craig, Ed Roebuck, and Karl Spooner; outfielders Carl Furillo and Sandy Amoros; and catcher Al "Rube" Walker. It was a diverse group with fascinating personal histories.

Erskine pitched two no-hitters in his career, one in a rain-interrupted game against the Chicago Cubs at Brooklyn's Ebbets Field in 1952. Minutes before the game, Dodger announcer Vin Scully sat down next to Carl in the dugout. "I wonder what the little pill has in store for me today?" Carl wondered out loud.[1]

During a forty-four-minute rain delay, Carl played bridge in the clubhouse. He had just made a four-heart hand when he returned to the mound to complete the game and the no-hitter. News coverage of the game inspired bridge expert Charles Goren to re-create Carl's four-heart hand in his nationally syndicated column.

The guy who purchased Ransom Jackson's trophy tarpon didn't know it was reeled in by Ransom, peeking through the catch of the day, with Brooklyn Dodger teammates, left to right, Carl Furillo, Karl Spooner, Rube Walker (behind Spooner), Carl Erskine, and Roy Campanella. Ransom Jackson Collection.

Craig was a tall, lanky country boy from North Carolina who eventually became my roommate on the road. He joined the Dodgers halfway through the 1955 season, winning five games and beating the New York Yankees in the World Series. His twelve victories in 1956 were critical in the Dodgers winning the National League pennant.

Roebuck was a funny guy off the field but very serious on it. He was used almost exclusively in relief, starting only once in 460 career appearances over eleven years.

The left-handed Spooner broke into the majors with a bang near the end of the 1954 season. In his first game against the New York Giants, who had just clinched the pennant, Spooner pitched a shutout, striking out a record fifteen batters. He whiffed twelve in his second game, also a shutout. "We shoulda had Spoona soona!" Dodger fans yelled. By the spring of 1956, Spooner was making one last attempt to rebound from a shoulder injury.

The Cuban-born Amoros, a small, speedy outfielder, spoke broken English, so he didn't say much. You hardly knew he was around. He made the biggest statement of the 1955 World Series with his glove, streaking into the left-field corner at Yankees Stadium in the seventh game to grab a line-drive smash and turn it into a Series-saving double play. "A piece of baseball immortality," the *New York Times* called the catch that came with the tying runs on base and no outs in the sixth inning.[2]

Furillo was another quiet guy, somewhat of a loner. When we traveled, Carl usually sat by himself. He was a solid hitter and fantastic right fielder with a cannon for an arm. Nobody dared take an extra base on him.

Walker, an easygoing guy from North Carolina, started his career with the Cubs before joining the Dodgers as insurance at catcher in case Campy got hurt. He was subbing for the injured Campy in the decisive third game of the playoff series against the Giants in 1951 when Bobby Thomson hit his famous "shot heard 'round the world" home run in the bottom of the ninth inning to win the National League pennant.

As Campy navigated Biscayne Bay, the rest of us concentrated on snagging a tarpon. Somebody caught one, but it quickly broke the one-hundred-pound test line. Then I hooked and reeled in a five-foot-long, fifty-five-pounder.

On returning to shore, I was asked if I wanted to make a trophy of my prized catch.

"What will it cost?"

"A hundred and ten dollars. We'll stuff it and ship it to you."

That was a good deal. And it looked even better when I got the mounted tarpon, its mouth wide open and glistening silver body battling to break free.

For thirty years, this beauty adorned a wall in my office. It graced a bedroom wall for another ten years, spent a little time in the attic, and then several more years near the organ in our playroom. We dusted it off and placed it in the driveway for the yard sale.

This guy meandered up with his hands in his bib overall pockets. "Nice-looking fish you got there. What kind is it?"

"It's a tarpon."

"Oh, it is, huh?"

"Yeah, I caught it down in Miami."

"You did, huh? What you want for it?"

"How about fifteen bucks?"

"Well, I think that's about right."

Every time I look at a photograph of Campy and the gang on the fishing boat, I imagine the story the new owner of the tarpon is telling these days.

He probably has it prominently displayed above his fireplace at home.

"Boy, that's a good-looking fish," people tell him.

"Yeah, I caught that sucker down off the coast of Florida. That thing about broke my line. I fought him for an hour and a half."

If only he knew the rest of the story.

43

REMEMBERING "THE GALLOPING GHOST"

Memorabilia from my baseball career covers the walls of the den at my home in Athens, Georgia. There are Dodger and Cub pennant flags, baseball cards, and photographs of baseball greats known widely by their first name or nicknames. There's Jackie, Duke, Pee Wee, Campy, Stan the Man, Mr. Cub, and a picture of me shaking hands with a man everybody knew as Ike. There's nothing to show, however, for a football icon I shared a late afternoon with in 1952 at his apartment near Chicago's Wrigley Field—Harold "Red" Grange, the Galloping Ghost.

As a kid I saw scratchy, black-and-white newsreel films showing Red running over everybody and people referring to him like the other sports legends of the time—baseball's Babe Ruth, golf's Bobby Jones, boxing's Jack Dempsey, and Paavo Nurmi, long-distance runner. In fact, famed sportswriter Damon Runyon wrote: "This man Red Grange of Illinois is three or four men and a horse rolled into one for football purposes. He is Jack Dempsey, Babe Ruth, Al Jolson, Paavo Nurmi and Man O'War."[1]

When I was introduced to Red and invited over to his place after a game, I was in shock, not to mention awe. What did I do to deserve a private audience with the Galloping Ghost?

From 1923 to 1925 Red galloped for the University of Illinois. In a game against the University of Michigan for the national championship in 1924, Red scored six touchdowns, three in the first twelve minutes. This inspired Grantland Rice, the sportswriter who wrote a poem immortalizing the backfield of Notre Dame's 1924 football team as the Four Horsemen, to write:

> A streak of fire, a breath of flame
> Eluding all who reach and clutch;
> A gray ghost thrown into the game
> That rival hands may never touch;
> A rubber bounding, blasting soul
> Whose destination is the goal. [2]

On Thanksgiving Day 1925 Red made his debut with the Chicago Bears of the National Football League before a capacity crowd at Wrigley Field of thirty-six thousand, the largest in pro football history at the time. He went on a nineteen-game barnstorming tour with the Bears that showcased the NFL and gave it credibility as a major sports league.

Of all the Cub players, I still don't know why Red picked me. I never asked. Perhaps it was because I played three years of college football, but that was kids' stuff compared to what Red did. All I know is we talked three hours about sports. I was twenty-three years younger than Red, and it was mind blowing hearing him talk about old-time football and showing his own memorabilia.

Red was a practical man, as this quote suggests: "I played the only way I know how. If you have the football and eleven guys are after you, if you're smart, you'll run. It was no big deal." [3]

I was no Red Grange, but my approach was similar. "You catch the ball and you run with it," I once explained my understanding of football when I started playing in college. "If you see a guy on the other team with a ball, you tackle him. That's about it."

Baseball was no different. See the ball and hit it if you've got a bat, catch it if you're wearing a glove. If you can tag a guy out, tag him.

Football or baseball, it was no big deal—just like Red said.

Of course, spending one-on-one time with Red was a big deal. A photograph of us together on my den wall would be nice, but the imagery, and memory, of the Galloping Ghost is stronger with no picture.

44

SHOELESS JOE AND OTHER JACKSONS

Every week I get a half dozen letters asking for autographs. They come from all over the United States and sometimes from Japan, Germany, and the Czech Republic.

The letters received soon after my last game in 1959 typically started, "I remember seeing you play."

Later on, it was, "My father said you were a really good player."

Now, the letters begin, "My grandfather used to watch you play."

One writer touched all the bases: "I grew up a Cubs fan hearing stories from my Grandpa and Dad about their favorite players. My Grandpa idolized your play."

I've kept the best ones, filling four scrapbooks.

One request I got was intended for Randy Jackson, a judge on a popular American television show: "I'm a big fan and watch *American Idol* all the time. Could you please send me an autographed picture or something?" Since I was the wrong guy, I replied, "He's a higher pay grade than I am. Sorry."

Another case of mistaken identity was this letter to Randy Jackson, a six-foot-five and 250-pound tackle in the National Football League from 1967 to 1974: "Mr. Jackson, I am a long-time fan of yours and the Chicago Bears. You were a great offensive lineman and a team leader."

One of the funniest is a letter addressed to "Shoeless Joe" Jackson, saying "what a raw deal" I got in the World Series. Jackson was banned after he was accused of helping to fix the 1919 World Series. He died in

1951. I answered, "You're going to have to go to a higher power than me to get an autograph."

When I was playing for the Chicago Cubs and still single, a West Chicago woman wrote that her four-year-old son, an avid Cubs fan, heard on the radio that I wasn't married. "So my youngster said to me, 'Mommie, why don't you marry Handsome Ransom and, then, I'll have a Daddy again.'"

More recently, I heard from Evelyn Lee, a budding collector. "My activities director suggested I start a hobby so I decided to write to baseball players for their autographs," she explained, adding: "I am eighty-seven."

A guy named Robert wrote: "Dear Mr. Johnson: I am a huge fan of yours and I would be proud and honored if you would sign and date this baseball for my personal collection. Mr. Johnson, could you add Ransom to the ball?"

Steve Stout, sports editor of a newspaper in Urbana, Ohio, asked me to sign and write a personal note on a photo for a friend's five-year-old son named James Ransom. The friend happened to be Clancy Brown, an actor best known for playing the evil Captain Byron Hadley in the movie *The Shawshank Redemption*. "He is a huge baseball fan," Stout said.

Rick Parker of Owasso, Oklahoma, an ex-Marine studying to be a registered nurse, wrote, "I'd rather be pitching in Yankee Stadium, but I do what I can do!" He already had the autographs of baseball greats Mickey Mantle, Warren Spahn, Stan Musial, Hank Aaron, and Roger Maris, but "it was the everyday players I really liked getting autographs from as they seemed to take a bigger interest in me as a young boy who loved baseball."

Roseann Sarvis of Newburgh, New York, wrote on behalf of her father who was too shy to ask for an autograph. "He talks about those days like they were yesterday," Roseann said. "My Dad's old baseball cards are long gone so I can't send you one of those to sign but if it's not too much trouble, I have enclosed a baseball and a return envelope. I would really appreciate it if you could sign the baseball and mention your nickname 'Ransom' so that I could give it to Dad."

In 2007 I got a poignant letter from the children of Doug Jacobsen—Juli, Phil, and Brad. "We grew up in a family that measured time by the seasons," they said. "Not spring, summer, winter or fall, but by the baseball seasons. It was either baseball or it was the 'off-season.'

"Some families might know their birth year by their astrological sign or Chinese animal, but even our birth years were marked by baseball."

Juli was born in 1965, the year of the Dodgers, and the boys in 1967, the year of the Cardinals, and 1968, the year of the Tigers.

"Our father is a great man and a hero to his kids. This year we thought it would be great if our hero heard from his heroes to wish him a happy birthday. His heroes are baseball players. His hero is you!"

The letter continued:

"Our dad grew up in a small Utah town called Vernal. Each year during the World Series his family would drive three hours to Salt Lake City, rent a hotel room and watch fuzzy, static images of the world's greatest game.

"Each time he took us out to the ballgame he would tell us about these trips and his childhood. Through baseball we got to know our dad."

Their father, Doug, had a sixty-fifth birthday coming up, so they enclosed a piece of paper to sign and "tell him about your favorite moment, time at bat or just sitting on the bench as one of his heroes sitting next to and playing against his other heroes."

Many letters relate childhood experiences.

"I recall hearing on TV one evening that you had been traded to the Dodgers," Don Peterson of Louisburg, Kansas, wrote in 2009. "I ran through the house yelling that the Cubs couldn't do that. I wrote the Cubs protesting the trade, and received a letter from Wid Matthews, director of player personnel, explaining their decision. I had it framed and placed on my wall for many years."

Peterson followed up with a copy of Wid's classic response: "Please remember that we finished last, seventh, and sixth the last three years with Ransom Jackson in the lineup."

Thomas Cottone grew up in the Bensonhurst section of Brooklyn. "You have always been one of my baseball heroes and among my favorite Dodger players," he wrote in 2011. "As the years have slipped away, a child's dream of becoming a major leaguer has faded and has been replaced with the adult cares of the modern world. However, those rich and warm schoolyard memories dreaming that I was Randy Jackson in the 'big game' at Public School 186 remain."

I have never refused a request for an autograph. An incident described by Bill Benjamin of Evanston, Illinois, in a 2001 letter explains why.

One day Bill and his brother, Tom, were waiting outside the Cub locker room at Wrigley Field to get autographs. Two of the players "barely acknowledged a group of us young boys with pencils and scorecards held in hands with arms outstretched. Your response was quite different."

As Bill recalls, I was sitting in an open convertible waiting for teammate Harry Chiti. "Not only did you take time to smile and talk to two young fans, but you actually invited us to sit inside the car while you waited for Harry. When Harry appeared, we all continued to talk for what seemed like hours.

"At the time, you no doubt gave that moment little significance. But to two young Cub fans, it was enormous and something I obviously have never forgotten nor ever will."

Joe Distelheim of Hilton Head Island, South Carolina, wrote in 2011 to tell me I was his favorite player even though he grew up in Chicago White Sox territory on the South Side. Joe's first baseball uniform was a T-shirt with my number two stenciled on the back by his mother.

"My friends and I would buy grandstand seats for $1.25, work our way down toward the field when the Andy Frain ushers weren't looking, and sneak into the box seats right behind third base when the ushers left after about the sixth inning. In those days, the '50s, the superstation hadn't yet made the Cubs a team with a national following; empty seats were plentiful.

"I remember that your first full year was 1951, my first year as a fan. I recall that the perennial second-division Cubs surprisingly hung in with the Dodgers for the first half of the next season. I remember that Bill Serena was your competition at third base, that Paul Minner was a great-hitting pitcher, that Bert Wilson used to call the games on WIND radio, that Eddie Miksis had a reputation for using words I wasn't supposed to know as an innocent youngster. . . .

"My baseball passion is one of the best memories of my childhood. Maybe it will give you a smile to know that you were a big part of that."

A doctor friend of mine in Athens, Georgia, also grew up on Chicago's South Side. We were playing golf one day when he mentioned his favorite player was outfielder Andy Pafko. "I used to sneak in and watch batting practice," he said. "That's all I wanted to see—Andy Pafko."

Andy was a star outfielder for the Cubs from 1943 until 1951 when he was traded to the Dodgers.

I wrote Andy, asking for an autographed photo I could give my friend. About two weeks later I got a large envelope back from Andy and headed straight to the doctor's office. When he saw Andy's picture, he had tears in his eyes. "Best wishes and thanks for remembering," Andy wrote.

"I know just where I'm going to put it," the doctor said. "Above the fireplace in my den."

Jim McGrath of Staten Island, New York, was a fire chief when he wrote me in 2001. He grew up in the Bay Ridge section of Brooklyn. He lived on Ridge Boulevard, between Ninety-First and Ninety-Second streets.

"If I remember correctly, you lived on 91st Street just a few houses below Ridge Blvd.," Jim said. "My friends and I were constantly bothering you for your autograph and tips on how we could be better Little Leaguers. You always took the time to stop and talk to us and sign our scraps of paper. . . . I no longer have the scraps of paper but I do have the memories."

Memories are life, far more important than any scrap of paper. Keep the cards, letters, photos, and scraps of paper coming. They bring back fond memories for me, too.

When I'm no longer around to answer, you'll be redirected to the same higher power handling matters for another ex-ballplayer named Jackson—Shoeless Joe.

45

WHERE HAVE ALL THE JACKIES GONE?

If Jackie Robinson and I came along today, neither one of us would play pro baseball. I would take a crack at the Professional Golfers' Association tour and Jackie would be a first-round National Football League draft pick and likely become an all-pro running back.

My decision to golf would be no big deal. But losing Jackie would've altered the course of baseball that's currently losing the best African American athletes to football and basketball.

In 2015 African Americans accounted for only sixty-eight or 7.8 percent of the 868 players on Opening Day rosters and inactive lists of Major League Baseball's thirty teams, *USA Today* reports.[1]

Meanwhile, there were 230 foreign-born players or 26.5 percent from seventeen countries and territories. With eighty-three players, the Dominican Republic led the way, followed by Venezuela, sixty-five, and Cuba, eighteen.

The highest percentage of African Americans in the majors was 18.7 percent in 1981, according to a detailed study by Mark Armour and Daniel R. Levitt of the Society of American Baseball Research.[2]

From 1950 when I broke into the big leagues through 1959 when I retired, the number of African Americans climbed from 1.7 to 8.8 percent and Latinos from 3 to 6.5 percent.[3]

This demographic data is scrutinized and analyzed every year around April 15, the day in 1947 when Jackie Robinson broke organized baseball's color barrier.

The 2013 movie *42* chronicled the story and heightened awareness of fewer African Americans playing baseball from youth leagues to the majors. The situation prompted MLB to form a task force that's looking for ways to solve the problem.

Currently, MLB is focusing on expanding existing urban leagues and academies; improving and modernizing coaching; and aggressively marketing African American players such as C.C. Sabathia, a pitcher selected by the Cleveland Indians in the first round of the 1998 amateur draft.

"If I had a choice, I would have had to go to college to play football, because my mom couldn't afford to pay whatever the percent was of my baseball scholarship," Sabathia says.[4]

"Baseball in the United States has become a sport for the rich," says LaTroy Hawkins, an African American pitcher with twenty-plus seasons in the majors.[5]

Eric Davis, one of the top African American stars in the 1980s and 1990s, cites the lack of father figures in the black community as the primary cause for the decline. "It's usually your grandfather, your uncle or father who puts that glove in your hand and says, 'Let's go play catch,'" Davis says, noting: "We've taken the father out of the equation for a lot of black kids and it's putting pressure on these mothers to raise these kids—and then try to teach baseball."[6]

Sabathia agrees. "Baseball's a sport where you learn how to play catch with your dad," he said. "There's a lot of single-parent homes in the inner city, so it's hard to get kids to play."[7]

Even comedian Chris Rock, who calls himself "an endangered species—a black baseball fan," has weighed in with a monologue on the subject.[8]

Rock points out that players from the Dominican Republic dominate baseball. "And the only equipment they have is twigs for bats, diapers for gloves, and Haitians for bases. It's not the money."[9]

He blames the game. "It's old-fashioned and stuck in the past. You've got the white-haired, white guy announcers. You've got cheesy old organ music at the games. Where's the Beats by Dre?

"It's the only game where there's a right way to play the game—the white way. The way it was played a hundred years ago when only whites were allowed to play.

"Black people don't like to look back. Throwback Thursday is about as far back as black people like to go.

"Maybe if baseball gets a little hipper, a little cooler, just a little more black, the future can change," Rock concludes. "But till then blacks and baseball just ain't a good match any more."[10]

Rock is paid to be funny and provocative. His quips deserve serious consideration.

There's nothing wrong with the game that can't be fixed by a few African American superstars like we had in the 1950s—Jackie, Willie Mays, Henry Aaron, Frank Robinson, and Ernie Banks.

All of them grew up in cities—Jackie in the Los Angeles area, Willie in Birmingham, Henry in Mobile, Frank in Oakland, and Ernie in Dallas. They had to overcome racial and economic hurdles far worse than today.

The decline of African Americans in baseball really comes down to space, money, and frankly, the desire to do other things.

Baseball is a long season and very expensive for kids. Parents have to buy their equipment—a uniform, shoes, an aluminum bat, gloves for fielding and hitting, a batting helmet, and a special bag to carry it around. There's also the transportation costs of traveling to various playing fields, some of them far away in other cities. Across the United States there are thousands of recreational parks with multiple baseball fields but seldom are they located in the inner city.

Rock is right when he says the game has slowed down while the world has sped up. Compared to basketball and football, baseball is a slow sport, especially for kids learning to play it.

It's not a game like basketball that you can play by yourself in a driveway, school playground, or at the end of a cul-de-sac. Baseball requires space and a group of kids to play.

The biggest problem with Little League baseball is the disparity in playing time between the best players and others on a team. No kid is going to improve sitting on the bench or batting once a game. Youth baseball should be about playing, not winning.

I can trace my steps to the majors back to one summer when I was thirteen and our junior high school field was taken over on Saturdays by high school boys playing softball. There weren't enough of them for a game, so they picked several younger guys to join them.

We lined up hoping to be chosen by one of the two team captains, who were the biggest and the best of the high schoolers. As the summer progressed, I went from being one of the last players selected to first or second. That gave me the confidence needed to continue playing.

When I coached Little League, I let everyone play. That's the only way for kids to get better and enjoy the game as they get older.

There are plenty of other things for kids, black and white, to do nowadays. They've got iPads, iPhones, and computers to play video games and send selfie photos and text messages to each other. They can put on a Beats headset and listen to rap music or a Chris Rock comedy routine. There's soccer, tennis, golf, and karate or they can sit in front of a big-screen, high-definition television at home and watch others play sports 24/7.

Baseball was truly the national pastime when Jackie and I got out of college. Little attention was paid to the NFL and National Basketball Association (NBA). People probably knew more about the Phillips 66ers, an amateur team sponsored by the Phillips Petroleum Company, than the Fort Wayne Pistons of the NBA.

As a teenager I was beating adults in golf tournaments, so it stands to reason that it was my best sport, not baseball or football, which I played in college. I became a major-league baseball player by accident.

Jackie picked baseball over football even though it was his worst at UCLA where he starred in four sports. Football was his best.

He led the nation in punt return average in both 1939 and 1940, his career average of 18.8 yards per return fourth best in NCAA history. As a junior in 1939 he averaged 11.4 yards per carry and in 1940, his senior year, he led UCLA in rushing, passing, total offense, scoring, and punt returns.

Jackie played baseball only one year at UCLA, and he batted .097. He had the talent and determination to go on and become baseball's greatest, most versatile player and blaze a trail for other African Americans to follow.

It's doubtful Jackie would be surprised that there are now more foreign-born players than African Americans in MLB.

During the Brooklyn Dodgers' tour of Japan in 1956, Jackie was asked if baseball was more popular in Japan or the United States. "At seven the other morning we were going out to play golf," he said. "We passed a place where four baseball games were going on in one lot. Where in America would you see that at seven a.m. in November?"[11]

Jackie could see MLB changing as far back as 1956. It may well be that future Jackies will come from other countries.

STATISTICS

Bats right, throws right / Height: 6-1 / Weight: 180 lbs. / Born: February 10, 1926, Little Rock, Arkansas

Year	CLUB	LGE	G	AB	R	H	2B	3B	HR	RBI	SB	BB	SO	BA
1948	Des Moines	WL	132	485	100	156	31	9	6	76	7	80	83	.322
1949	Los Angeles	PCL	14	44	6	14	3	0	2	6	0	4	7	.318
1949	Oklahoma City	TL	138	524	89	156	22	13	19	109	11	65	74	.298
1950	Springfield	IL	117	494	78	134	22	5	20	68	4	62	41	.315
1950	Chicago	NL	34	111	13	25	4	3	3	6	4	7	25	.225
1951	Chicago	NL	145	557	78	153	24	6	16	76	14	47	44	.275
1952	Chicago	NL	116	379	44	88	8	5	9	34	6	27	42	.232
1953	Chicago	NL	139	498	61	142	22	8	19	66	8	42	61	.285
1954	Chicago	NL	126	484	77	132	17	6	19	67	2	44	55	.273
1955	Chicago	NL	138	499	73	132	13	7	21	70	0	58	58	.265
1956	Brooklyn	NL	101	307	37	84	15	7	8	53	2	28	38	.274
1957	Brooklyn	NL	48	131	7	26	1	0	2	16	0	9	20	.198
1958	Los Angeles	NL	35	65	8	12	3	0	1	4	0	5	10	.185
1958	Cleveland	AL	29	91	7	22	3	1	4	13	0	3	18	.242
1959	Cleveland	AL	3	7	0	1	0	0	0	0	0	0	1	.143
1959	Chicago	NL	41	74	7	18	5	1	1	10	0	11	10	.243
Minors			401	1478	273	460	78	27	47	259	22	211	205	.312
Majors			955	3203	412	835	115	44	103	415	36	281	382	.261

NOTES

INTRODUCTION

1. HBO Films, Alec Baldwin, *The Lost Ballparks of Major League Baseball*. https://m.youtube.com/watch?v=FJMCa-8Teb4.

3. ACCIDENTAL BIG LEAGUER

1. *Sporting News*, May 19, 1954, 1.
2. OrangeWhoopass.com, September 10, 2001, http://www.orangewhoopass.com/2001/09/10/bibb-falka-texas-original/.
3. OrangeWhoopass.com, September 10, 2001.
4. *Helena (AR) World*, date in 1947 and page number unknown for story titled "Local Youth Is Writing Sports History at Texas University."
5. "Local Youth."
6. "Local Youth."

4. THE AMAZING BOBBY LAYNE

1. Art Donovan on *The Tonight Show* with Johnny Carson, https://m.youtube.com/watch?v=7HDRLnoAY9E.
2. *Sports Illustrated*, Fall 1995 Extra Issue, cover.

5. FROM CONROE TO THE CUBS

1. *Houston Press*, August 1, 1947, 24.
2. *Victoria (TX) Advocate*, January 11, 1949, 52.
3. *Victoria Advocate*, January 11, 1949, 52.
4. Newspaper unknown. Story by Edgar Munzel titled "Bumper 'Crop' Seen for Cubs" published in late October 1947.

6. TRAINING WITH THE GOATS

1. Jack Brickhouse with Jack Rosenberg and Ned Colletti, *Thanks for Listening!* (South Bend, IN: Diamond Communications, 1986), 61.
2. Jim Vitti, *The Cubs on Catalina* (Darien, CT: Settefrati, 2003), 33.
3. Bill Veeck with Ed Linn, *Veeck as in Wreck: The Autobiography of Bill Veeck* (Chicago: University of Chicago Press, 2001), 296.
4. Veeck, *Veeck as in Wreck*, 297.
5. Veeck, *Veeck as in Wreck*, 297.
6. *Los Angeles Times*, May 17, 1953, B7.
7. Nan Holloman, *This One and That One: The True Life Story of BoBo "No-Hit" Holloman* (Athens, GA: Nan Holloman, 1975), 33–34.

7. FIELD OF DREAMS

1. Henry Ford Museum, https://www.thehenryford.org/exhibits/showroom/1948/tucker.html.
2. Henry Ford Museum.

8. ALMOST THERE

1. Grant Dunlap, *Kill the Umpire* (Mount Pleasant, TX: Nortex, 1998), 11.
2. Dunlap, *Kill the Umpire*, 60–61.
3. *Daily Oklahoman*, May 14, 1949, 9.
4. *Oklahoma City Times*, August 10, 1949, 24.

9. NEW KID IN TOWN

1. *Sporting News*, May 17, 1950, 10.
2. *Chicago Sun-Times*, May 28, 1950, 23.
3. *Chicago Sun-Times*, May 6, 1950, 28.
4. *Chicago Sun-Times*, May 6, 1950, 28.
5. *Chicago Sun-Times*, May 6, 1950, 28.
6. *Chicago Herald-American*, May 6, 1950, page number unknown.
7. *Sporting News*, May 17, 1950, 10.
8. *Sporting News*, May 17, 1950, 10.
9. *Boston Herald*, September 13, 1950, 22.

11. WHO'S ON THIRD?

1. *Chicago American,* January 12, 1954, 28.
2. *Chicago Sun-Times*, March 4, 1951, 74.
3. *Sporting News*, March 10, 1948, 19.
4. *Chicago Daily News*, date and page number unknown for Howard Roberts story titled "Lack of Spirit Retards Ransom."
5. Roberts, "Lack of Spirit."
6. Roberts, "Lack of Spirit."
7. *Chicago Sun-Times,* May 20, 1951, 74.
8. *Chicago Sun-Times,* May 20, 1951, 74.
9. *Chicago Herald-American*, July 5, 1951, 33.
10. *Chicago Daily News*, date and page number unknown for John P. Carmichael's Barber Shop column.
11. *Chicago Daily News*, date and page number unknown for story by Neil R. Gazel titled "N.L. Managers Eye Cubs' Jackson with Envy."
12. Gazel, "Managers Eye Cubs' Jackson."
13. Gazel, "Managers Eye Cubs' Jackson."
14. Abbott and Costello, "Who's on First," YouTube, https://m.youtube.com/watch?v=kTcRRaXV-fg.

12. THE POWER OF CHOCOLATE DONUTS

1. *New York Times*, August 10, 1999, C20.
2. *Chicago Tribune*, May 19, 1951, 30.

13. BATTING BEHIND THE MAYOR

1. Jack Brickhouse with Jack Rosenberg and Ned Colletti, *Thanks for Listening!* (South Bend, IN: Diamond Communications, 1986), 217.
2. *New York Times*, August 10, 1999, C20.

15. FIRE AND MONEY

1. *Sporting News*, April 29, 1953, 7.
2. *Sporting News*, April 29, 1953, 7.
3. *Chicago Daily News*, date and page number unknown for a Howard Roberts story titled "Lack of Spirit Retards Ransom."
4. *Sporting News*, August 1, 1951, 9.
5. *Tucson Daily Citizen*, February 27, 1952, 21.
6. *Chicago American*, January 12, 1954, 28.
7. *Chicago Sun-Times*, May 20, 1951, 74.
8. *Sporting News,* August 1, 1951, 9.
9. *Chicago Daily News*, July 8, 1953, 34.
10. *Sporting News,* July 29, 1953, 6.

16. MAKING WAVES ON WAVELAND

1. *Chicago Sun-Times*, April 18, 1954, 66.
2. *Chicago Daily News*, exact date and page number unknown for April 1954 story by Howard Roberts titled "Jackson in Fast Start."
3. *Lawton (OK) Constitution*, date and page number unknown for Lew Johnson's column in 1954 titled "Papa Pleased with Ransom's Bat."
4. *Sporting News*, July 14, 1954, 19.

17. ONE OF A KIND

1. *Chicago Tribune*, Mary 13, 1955, part 4, 1.
2. Jack Brickhouse with Jack Rosenberg and Ned Colletti, *Thanks for Listening!* (South Bend, IN: Diamond Communications, 1986), 131.
3. Brickhouse, *Thanks for Listening!*, 131.

19. WASTING AWAY IN WRIGLEYVILLE

1. *Chicago Tribune, 100 Years of Wrigley Field*, "'Toothpick Sam' and His Historic No-Hitter," March 28, 2014, YouTube, https://m.youtube.com/watch?v=3rpUqf3dW5M.

2. Gaylon H. White, *The Bilko Athletic Club: The Story of the 1956 Los Angeles Angels* (Lanham, MD: Rowman & Littlefield, 2014), 258.

3. *Chicago Tribune*, August 28, 1975, section 4, page 3.

4. *Sporting News*, July 24, 1971, 20.

5. *Chicago Sun-Times*, January 7, 1951, 72.

6. *Chicago Sun-Times*, January 7, 1951, 72.

7. *Sporting News*, March 16, 1952, 6.

8. *Sporting News*, March 16, 1952, 6.

9. *Sporting News*, March 16, 1952, 6.

10. *Los Angeles Times*, March 31, 1953, C2.

11. Quoted in the *Chicago Tribune*, March 31, 1997, section 7, page 8.

12. *Chicago Tribune*, March 31, 1997, section 7, page 8.

13. *Chicago Tribune*, March 31, 1997, section 7, page 8.

14. Society of American Baseball Research, http://sabr.org/bioproj/person/3c15c318.

15. *Sporting News*, April 8, 1953, 19.

20. IF YOU CAN'T BEAT 'EM, JOIN 'EM

1. *Chicago Daily News*, December 7, 1955, 64.

2. Newspaper unknown. Associated Press wire-service story titled "Dodgers Get Best of Jackson Deal," published around December 7, 1955.

3. *Chicago Daily News*, December 8, 1955, 47.

4. *Chicago Tribune*, December 21, 1955, 34.

5. Newspaper unknown.

6. Newspaper unknown.

7. *Sporting News*, January 18, 1956, 4.

8. *Sporting News*, January 18, 1956, 4.

9. Newspaper unknown.

21. JACKIE AND ME

1. *New York Times*, December 8, 1955, 54.

2. Roger Kahn, *The Boys of Summer* (New York: Signet, 1973), 358.
3. *Sporting News*, July 18, 1956, 10.
4. *Greeley (CO) Tribune*, March 9, 1956, 15.
5. *Greeley Tribune*, March 9, 1956, 15.
6. *Sporting News*, July 18, 1956, 10.
7. *Lawton (OK) Constitution*, April 3, 1956, 8.
8. *Sporting News*, April 25, 1956, 9.
9. *Sporting News*, July 18, 1956, 10.
10. *New York Daily Mirror*, June 30, 1956, 40.
11. *New York Daily News*, June 30, 1956, 26.
12. *New York Post*, June 30, 1956, 40.
13. *New York Post*, June 30, 1956, 40.

22. A MASTERPIECE (AND A FLUKE)

1. Bill Veeck with Ed Linn, *Veeck as in Wreck: The Autobiography of Bill Veeck* (Chicago: University of Chicago Press, 2001), 297.
2. Veeck, *Veeck as in Wreck*, 297.
3. Veeck, *Veeck as in Wreck*, 297.
4. *ESPN Classic SportsCentury*, http://espn.go.com/classic/biography/s/larsen_don.html.
5. *ESPN Classic SportsCentury*.
6. *New York Times*, October 8, 1956, A1.
7. *New York Times*, October 8, 1956, A1.

23. KINGS IN JAPAN

1. *Sport* magazine, April 1957, 26–27.
2. National Baseball Hall of Fame, http://baseballhall.org/hof/drysdale-don.
3. *Pantagraph* (Bloomington, IL), October 23, 1956, 13.
4. *Sport* magazine, April 1957, 92.
5. *Sporting News*, November 21, 1956, 7.

24. BUMMER OF A SEASON

1. *Lawton (OK) Constitution*, date in early 1954 and page number unknown for story titled "Lawton's Jackson Praised by Cobb."
2. *New York Times*, April 4, 1957, 43.
3. *Kansas City Times*, April 12, 1957, 1.
4. *Kansas City Times*, April 12, 1957, 1.
5. *Kansas City Times*, April 12, 1957, 1.
6. *Los Angeles Times*, May 14, 1961, H1.
7. *New York Herald-Tribune*, April 13, 1957, section 3, 3.
8. *Sporting News*, July 31, 1957, 15.
9. *Sporting News*, September 25, 1957, 8.

25. THE DAY THE MUSIC DIED

1. Vin Scully video clip, http://twitpic.com/ec221d.
2. Vin Scully video clip.
3. *Moberly (MO) Monitor-Index*, November 19, 1963, 8.
4. *Moberly (MO) Monitor-Index*, November 19, 1963, 8.

26. STAR WATCHING IN L.A.

1. *Los Angeles Times*, January 15, 1958, C2.
2. *Los Angeles Times*, January 15, 1958, C2.
3. *Sporting News*, January 29, 1958, 5.
4. Don Drysdale with Bob Verdi, *Once a Bum, Always a Dodger* (New York: St. Martin's, 1990), 71.
5. Steve Delsohn, *True Blue: The Dramatic History of the Los Angeles Dodgers, Told by the Men Who Lived It* (New York: HarperCollins, 2001), 24.
6. *Los Angeles Times*, April 19, 1958, A1.
7. Delsohn, *True Blue*, 25.
8. Drysdale, *Once a Bum*, 69.

27. DETOUR TO CLEVELAND

1. *Chicago Sun-Times*, August 5, 1958, 50.

2. *Cleveland Plain Dealer*. Date and page number unknown for Hal Lebovitz story titled "Jackson 'Big Steal' of '58."

28. BACK WHERE I STARTED

1. *Los Angeles Times*, August 21, 1958, C8.
2. *Chicago American*, October 12, 1959, 15.
3. *Chicago American*, October 12, 1959, 15.
4. *Chicago American*, October 12, 1959, 15.

30. I'M NO JOE

1. Jack Brickhouse with Jack Rosenberg and Ned Colletti, *Thanks for Listening!* (South Bend, IN: Diamond Communications, 1986), 62.
2. Brickhouse, *Thanks for Listening!*, 62.
3. Brickhouse, *Thanks for Listening!*, 62.
4. Brickhouse, *Thanks for Listening!*, 64.

31. MY FRIEND, DAD

1. *Princeton Alumni Weekly*, February 6, 1948.
2. *Lawton (OK) Constitution*. Date and page number unknown for Lew Johnson's column in early 1954 titled "Lawton's Jackson Praises Hack."
3. Publication unknown. Quote on page 43 of story by Edgar Munzel titled "High, Wide—and Ransom."
4. *Sporting News*, April 29, 1953, 7.
5. *Sporting News*, April 29, 1953, 7.

33. MY FIRST LOVE

1. *Lamesa (TX) Daily Reporter*, March 18, 1951, 4.
2. *Lamesa Daily Reporter*, March 18, 1951, 4.
3. *Lamesa Daily Reporter*, March 18, 1951, 4.
4. *Chicago American*. Date and page number unknown for James Enright story in late 1953 or early 1954 titled "Randy Quits Golf, Finds It Hurt His Hitting."

5. Enright, "Randy Quits Golf."

6. Enright, "Randy Quits Golf."

7. Nan Holloman, *This One and That One: The True Life Story of BoBo "No-Hit" Holloman* (Athens, GA: Nan Holloman, 1975), 68.

34. PILGRIMAGE TO WRIGLEY FIELD

1. *Vineline* (Chicago Cubs newsletter), April 2011.

35. ONE FOR THE BOOK

1. *Sporting News*, August 1, 1951, 12.

2. *Chicago Tribune*, July 27, 1950, part 4, 1.

3. *Chicago Tribune*, July 27, 1950, part 4, 1.

4. *Chicago Tribune*, August 27, 1950, part 2, 7.

5. *Chicago Tribune*, August 27, 1950, part 2, 7.

6. *Chicago Tribune*, July 29, 1950, part 2, 1.

7. *Sporting News*, July 25, 1951, 9.

8. Grant Dunlap, *Kill the Umpire* (Mount Pleasant, TX: Nortex, 1998), 97.

36. THE MAN FROM MARS

1. *Sporting News*, March 28, 1956, 16.

2. *Daily Republican* (Monongahela, PA), June 17, 1955, 2.

3. *Charleroi (PA) Mail*, June 28, 1955, 11.

4. *Charleroi Mail*, July 11, 1955, 10.

5. *Sporting News*, April 11, 1956, 19.

6. *Charleroi Mail*, April 2, 1956, 7.

7. *Charleroi Mail*, May 2, 1956, 11.

8. *Sporting News*, April 11, 1956, 19.

9. *Sporting News*, April 11, 1956, 19.

37. MY ROOMIES

1. George W. Hilton, *The Annotated Baseball Stories of Ring W. Lardner* (Stanford, CA: Stanford University Press, 1995), 339.

2. BaseballLibrary.com, http://www.baseballlibrary.com/ballplayers/player. php?name=Ping_Bodie_1887.

3. *Chicago Sun-Times*, June 1, 1953, 45.

4. *Chicago Sun-Times*, June 4, 1953, 51.

5. *Chicago Sun-Times*, June 5, 1953, 47.

6. *Chicago Sun-Times*, June 2, 1953, 37.

7. Eddie Gold and Art Ahrens, *The New Era Cubs* (Chicago: Bonus Books, 1985), 65.

8. *Chicago Sun-Times*, June 3, 1953, 52.

9. MajorLeagueBaseball.com, http://m.cubs.mlb.com/news/article/ 2481925/.

10. George Gobel, Dean Martin, and Bob Hope on *The Tonight Show* with Johnny Carson, http://youtu.be/FyPxUA-Ik1o.

38. OF POWER PITCHERS AND POWDER PUFFS

1. *Knuckleball!* A film written, produced, and directed by Ricki Stern and Annie Sundberg (New York: Break Thru Films in association with Major League Baseball Productions, 2012).

2. *Knuckleball!*

3. *Knuckleball!*

4. *Bangor Daily News*, July 18, 1997, 99.

5. *Knuckleball!*

6. Society of American Baseball Research Biography Project, http://sabr. org/bioproj/person/b12cbf39.

7. Roger Kahn, *The Boys of Summer* (New York: Signet, 1973), 124.

8. Kahn, *Boys of Summer*, 124.

9. *Sporting News*, November 12, 1947, 11.

10. BilkoAthleticClub.com, http://www.bilkoathleticclub.com/blog/of-bilko-konerko-and-wilhelm/.

11. *New York Times*, October 31, 1996, D21.

12. *Chicago Tribune*, July 25, 1981, section 1, 7.

13. *New York Times*, October 31, 1996, D21.

39. THE CHEATING GAME

1. Dan Stephenson, *Richie Ashburn: A Baseball Life*, DVD, written and produced by Dan Stephenson, narrated by Harry Kalas (New York: Arts Alliance America LLC, 2008).
2. *Sporting News*, August 29, 1956, 24.
3. *New York Times*, February 7, 2007, A16.
4. *Sporting News*, August 29, 1956, 24.
5. *Sporting News*, August 29, 1956, 24.

40. HEAVEN ON EARTH

1. *Sporting News*, November 11, 1953, 18.
2. *Chicago Sun-Times*, June 24, 1953, 59.
3. *Chicago Sun-Times*, June 24, 1953, 59.
4. *Chicago Sun-Times*, June 24, 1953, 59.
5. *Chicago Tribune*, December 8, 1962, section 1, 14.
6. *Sporting News*, August 22, 1988, 21.
7. *Sporting News*, August 8, 1988, 14.
8. *Chicago Tribune*, August 29, 1988, section 4, 4.
9. *Chicago Tribune*, August 29, 1988, section 4, 4.
10. *Sporting News*, August 22, 1988, 6.
11. *Sporting News*, August 22, 1988, 21.
12. *Sporting News*, August 22, 1988, 21.

41. THE BAT THAT GLOWED

1. *New York Times*, March 8, 1990, D25.

42. A FISHING TALE THAT'S MOSTLY TRUE

1. Society of American Baseball Research, http://sabr.org/bioproj/person/2af3b16d.
2. *New York Times*, June 28, 1992, 32.

43. REMEMBERING "THE GALLOPING GHOST"

1. *Columbus Dispatch*, October 31, 2014, http://buckeyextra.dispatch.com/content/stories/2014/10/31/gameday/history.html.

2. *Chicago Tribune*, October 10, 2014, http://www.chicagotribune.com/news/history/ct-red-grange-flashback-1012-20141012-story.html#page=1.

3. *Columbus Dispatch*, October 31, 2014, http://buckeyextra.dispatch.com/content/stories/2014/10/31/gameday/history.html.

45. WHERE HAVE ALL THE JACKIES GONE?

1. *USA Today*, April 15, 2015, http://www.usatoday.com/story/sports/mlb/2015/04/14/mlb-diversity-percentage-of-african-american-players-remained-flat/25791993/.

2. Society of American Baseball Research (SABR), "Baseball Demographics, 1947–2012," http://sabr.org/bioproj/topic/baseball-demographics-1947-2012.

3. SABR, "Baseball Demographics."

4. *New York Times*, April 9, 2014, 18.

5. AtlantaBlackstar.com, April 8, 2015, http://atlantablackstar.com/2015/04/08/blacks-players-make-8-percent-major-league-baseball-getting-worse/.

6. IndyStar.com, June 21, 2014, http://www.indystar.com/story/sports/baseball/2014/06/21/ex-red-talks-declining-percentage-african-americans-baseball/11216039/.

7. *New York Times*, April 9, 2014, 18.

8. CBSSports.com, April 22, 2015, http://www.cbssports.com/mlb/eye-on-baseball/25159596/chris-rock-blacks-and-baseball-just-aint-a-good-match-anymore.

9. CBSSports.com, April 22, 2015.

10. CBSSports.com, April 22, 2015.

11. *Sporting News*, November 21, 1956, 7.

BIBLIOGRAPHY

Brickhouse, Jack, with Jack Rosenberg and Ned Colletti. *Thanks for Listening!* South Bend, IN: Diamond Communications, 1986.

Delsohn, Steve. *True Blue: The Dramatic History of the Los Angeles Dodgers, Told by the Men Who Lived It*. New York: HarperCollins, 2001.

Drysdale, Don, with Bob Verdi. *Once a Bum, Always a Dodger*. New York: St. Martin's, 1990.

Dunlap, Grant, *Kill the Umpire*. Mount Pleasant, TX: Nortex, 1998.

Gold, Eddie, and Art Ahrens. *The New Era Cubs*. Chicago: Bonus Books, 1985.

Hilton, George W. *The Annotated Baseball Stories of Ring W. Lardner*. Stanford, CA: Stanford University Press, 1995.

Holloman, Nan. *This One and That One: The True Life Story of BoBo "No-Hit" Holloman*. Athens, GA: Nan Holloman, 1975.

Kahn, Roger. *The Boys of Summer*. New York: Signet, 1973.

Veeck, Bill, with Ed Linn. *Veeck as in Wreck: The Autobiography of Bill Veeck*. Chicago: University of Chicago Press, 2001.

Vitti, Jim. *The Cubs on Catalina*. Darien, CT: Settefrati, 2003.

White, Gaylon H. *The Bilko Athletic Club: The Story of the 1956 Los Angeles Angels*. Lanham, MD: Rowman & Littlefield, 2014.

INDEX

ABOUT THE AUTHORS

Ransom Jackson was a professional baseball player for twelve years, ten in the majors. He played for the Chicago Cubs (1950–55 and 1959); the Dodgers in Brooklyn (1956–57) and Los Angeles (1958); and the Cleveland Indians (1958–59). He played in two Major League Baseball All-Star Games (1954 and 1955) and the 1956 World Series. In 955 major-league games, Jackson batted .261 with 103 home runs and 415 runs batted in.

Jackson played three years of college football, one at Texas Christian University and two at the University of Texas. He played in the 1945 and 1946 Cotton Bowl Classics on New Year's Day, the first for TCU and the second for Texas. He's the only player in Cotton Bowl history to play in successive years for different teams. Jackson also played three years of college baseball, leading the Southwest Conference in hitting all three seasons.

Jackson is a member of the University of Texas's cherished Longhorn Hall of Honor and the Brooklyn Dodgers Hall of Fame in recognition of him being the last Brooklyn player to hit a home run. He and his wife, Terry, live in Athens, Georgia.

Gaylon H. White is author of *The Bilko Athletic Club*, published in 2014 by Rowman & Littlefield. "One of the best sports books of 2014," Bruce Miles wrote in the *Chicago Daily Herald*.

The Los Angeles–born White was three years old in 1949 when Jackson briefly played at L.A.'s Wrigley Field for the Los Angeles Angels of the old Pacific Coast League. White didn't see Jackson play until he came to L.A. with the Dodgers in 1958, but he knew him long before that as "Handsome Ransom," all-star third baseman for his beloved Cubs.

White started his career as a sportswriter for the *Denver Post*, *Arizona Republic*, and *Oklahoma Journal* before becoming a speechwriter for top corporate executives. He has authored nearly one hundred articles in U.S. and international publications, many on baseball. He and his wife, Mary, live in Cartersville, Georgia.